roses

a care manual

Amanda Beales

LAUREL
GLEN

Publishing Director
Alison Goff
Creative Director
Keith Martin
Executive Editor
Julian Brown
Executive Art Editor
Mark Winwood
Design
Ruth Hope
Editor
Karen O'Grady
Production Controller
Sarah Scanlon
Picture Research
Liz Fowler
Photography
Mark Winwood

North American Edition
Publisher
Allen Orso
Managing Editor
JoAnn Padgett
Project Editor
Elizabeth McNulty

Published in the United States by
Laurel Glen Publishing,
An imprint of the Advantage Publishers Group
5880 Oberlin Drive, Suite 400
San Diego, CA 92121-4794
http://www.advantagebooksonline.com

ISBN 1-57145-644-9

Library of Congress Cataloging-in-Publication Data

Beales, Amanda.
    Roses : a care manual / Amanda Beales--North American ed.
    p. cm.
    Includes bibliographical references (p.).
    ISBN 1-57145-644-9
    1. Roses. 2. Rose culture. I. Title.

SB411 .B37 1999
635.9'33734--dc21

99-057593

Produced by Toppan
Printed in China

1 2 3 4 5   00 01 02 03 04

Acknowledgments

I aim to keep this short and mention
only a few people by name. All others
will hopefully realise how grateful I
have been for their support while
writing this book.

However, I would like to convey feelings
of gratitude to a few. To my Editor,
Karen O'Grady, for her patience and
dedication and Mark Winwood, for
portraying in pictures the ambience
of the rose, a magic that is difficult to
put into words. I thank my entire family
circle and fellow staff for all they have
done but in particular I owe my father
and mentor, Peter Beales, very much
for teaching me what I know and
my Mother and brother for their
encouragement. Lastly to the people
I dedicate this book to, those who
continually put up with so much so
that I may pursue my love of roses,
my husband David and children
Laura and Alexander.

Contents

Introduction

Introduction

Roses are a fundamental part of my life and always have been, not only in work but in leisure and, while I have no particular recollection of "falling for roses," it is likely that I was influenced as a very young child by the passion my father bestowed on them. I am told that as a baby I would lay in my buggy, guarded by the family dog, while my parents tended roses during the foundation years of my fathers now world-famous rose nursery. Roses have played a part in some key moments of my life; when christened at the tender age of just two months the vicar laid blooms of 'Zéphirine Drouhin,' the well known thornless Bourbon rose, on the font. It was the only rose still blooming in his garden (it was early winter). While I may have been thornless then, I am sure that the analogy was not quite so accurate when my father secretly had flowers of this and other roses flown in from Australia for my wedding day in late autumn! They made up a large part of my bouquet, which had a heavenly scent and was probably delicious also, to judge from photographs of the horse pulling our wedding day carriage. In turn, flowers of this beautiful rose graced the font at the christening of our daughter.

There are roses for every taste and nearly every possible situation, and flowers are available in many colors,

Amanda has always had a passion for roses and is responsible for introducing numerous new vareties.

perfumes, shapes, and sizes are available. Some are low growing; some have the capabilities of reaching the highest branches in the tallest of trees. Some flower for a long period, others for shorter times, and there are many with attractive hips and autumn foliage. There are roses that are in fashion and those that are relatively unknown. Throughout the rose directory in this book, I have tried to cover a good cross section of the many, many thousands of roses available, concentrating on an assortment of colors and habits, so that you, the reader can appreciate the diversity of the rose and be guided as to the best ones for your garden. In the earlier pages I discuss all that you will need to know when growing them in the garden, from preparing the soil to handling large, mature plants.

I love to indulge myself in the beauty and fragrance of roses; the naked garden of our newly acquired property is destined to be full of them, probably too full, for it is my intention to pack in as many different varieties as possible in as many ways as possible: mingling through the branches of trees, in hanging baskets, and in more conventional plantings.

I have a scheme in mind, lots of flowing, mingling color, and perfume with hips and interesting foliage. I have no doubt that I will continue to learn from my new garden companions, and I look forward to the delights that are ahead. Having worked in every aspect of rose growing, I have found that some of the most pleasurable times have been spent meeting fellow rose gardeners and learning to understand their common concerns and their desire to know more. I have drawn on this information and tried to respond to the needs of all rose gardeners throughout this book, whether needing just a little guidance in care and selection or, like me, starting from scratch with a new or previously neglected plot.

I hope that while dipping into the text, or enjoying Mark Winwood's superb photographs, you will pick up on the romance of the rose and come to share in it with me; it is at the same time addictive, fulfilling, and long lasting.

Amanda Beales

History

of the Rose

Early Beginnings

"Oh, no man knows through what wild centuries roves back the rose." Although not a rosarian, Walter de la Mare was accurate on this point, for no one can be absolutely certain of when the fascinating and complicated history of the rose began; although, from fossilized evidence found in areas of the northern hemisphere, we can assume that roses existed in some form in prehistoric times. Since then, their evolution into the roses we have today is intricately entwined with our own history, so it could be said that the history of the rose is the history of man's adoration of it.

Possibly one of the earliest references to the rose is in Homer's epic the *Iliad*, composed sometime in the 9th century BC, in which he tells that to celebrate victory over Hector, Achilles decorated his shield with roses and that Hector's body was anointed with rose oil. Roses are referred to in several instances in the Bible and it is very likely that they were grown in the Hanging Gardens of Babylon, one of the seven wonders of the world, which were created around 600 BC.

Ancient Civilizations

Representations of the flower are found on fresco paintings and discoveries dating back to the ancient Egyptian civilization. It is known that the rose was greatly admired by the Greeks who, it is believed, had examples of *Rosa gallica* and *R. damascena* imported from Persia; in fact the island of Rhodes took its name from the rose and coins, dating as far back as 400BC, depicting roses have been discovered there.

The Egyptians and Greeks certainly loved the rose but the Romans were fanatical about them. Believing them to be an aphrodisiac, they would thickly carpet the floor with them on the occasions of great banquets and festivities and would create garlands of them to be worn on the head. They also believed that they were a protection from drunkenness, and floated petals in their ale and wine. They even used rose petals to flavor food and in many

Roses depicted on a mosaic, portraying the preparation of a banquet from the House of Dionysos at Harrumetum (Indonesia).

cosmetic concoctions and medicinal potions. Roman author, Pliny recommended using roses in thirty-two different remedies and in his Natural History he mentions several different species and early hybrids including *Rosa alba*, *R. damascena*, and *R. canina* (a native of Europe). The Romans were so besotted with roses that they planted them in greenhouses surrounded by trenches which were continually filled with hot water in order to extend their flowering season. When this no longer worked they would trade with the Egyptians so that they could have blooms all year round. Sadly, with the fall of the Roman empire, the popularity of the rose also declined.

The Middle Ages

As medieval times began, the church rejected the rose as it was associated with pagan cults; in fact rose gardens were believed to be frequented by witches. But as the Dark Ages passed and the high Middle Ages commenced, the rose once again came into favor. Carvings and painting depicting the rose were commonplace and twenty-four varieties were fully described by the apothecary, John Parkinson (1569–1629) in his work *Paradisius terrsestris* (*The Earthy Paradise*).

One of the most famous of all roses, 'Rosa mundi,' dates back to this period in history. This beautiful striped gallica is said to have been named after the mistress of Henry II, fair Rosamund, whose sudden death may have been precipitated by the Queen.

The rose, of which 'Rosa mundi' is a sport, was also significant to medical sciene in medieval times: *Rosa gallica officinallis* is also known as the 'Apothecary's Rose,' for it and other similar roses were believed by the chemists of the day to possess healing powers. Exactly which illness was cured by this lovely rose is unknown.

In the 12th and 13th centuries, Crusaders traveled to the Middle East and brought back rose treasures to Europe, and France in particular. The Damask roses, arising from *Rosa damascena*, were cropped in Persia for the production of attar of the rose, or rose oil, used in the making of perfume. In fact, at least two of these roses bear the names of these centers of perfume making: 'Kazanlik' and 'Ispahan.' Literature of the time shows how well appreciated the rose was, and we know that it was grown in India, Kashmir, Morocco, Afghanistan, and elsewhere. Many of the roses collected by the Crusaders are still with us and went on to play an important part in the creation of modern-day roses.

Above: A portrayal of the third Crusade during which Philip Augustus of France and Richard I of England failed to recapture Jerusalem. Many roses were carried to Europe from distant shores during the Crusades.

Left: The extraction of "attar of the rose" or rose oil was complicated and demanded the invention of complicated distilleries.

The Rose in Religion

Throughout history, the rose has been symbolic. As early as 1200 BC the Persians used roses on staves and maces as religious emblems. Later they were used in the Christian church in adulation of the Virgin Mary; wreaths of roses were made in her honor and the ground would be strewn with rose petals for processions and Marian festivals. Rose windows, those circular stained glass insets with symmetrical petal-shaped panels, were included in the construction of cathedrals and other religious buildings. Roses were frequently carved on pew ends or formed in stone. It was believed that the white rose portrayed the purity of Mary, while the red rose portrayed the evil done to her son and acted as a reminder of his wounds.

The Heraldic Rose

These roses sprang and budded fair, and carried such a grace,
That kings of England in their armes afford them worthy place,
And flourish may these roses long that all the world may tell
The owners of these princely flowers in virtues doe excell.

ANON

The rose was also a frequent heraldic symbol, perhaps the two best known being the White Rose of York and the Red Rose of Lancaster. The Lancastrians' symbol was a red rose, *Rosa gallica officinalis*. The White Rose of York, believed to be *Rosa alba*, but said by some to be 'Alba Maxima,' was the symbol of Edward, Duke of York who defeated the Lancastrians at the battle of Mortimer's Cross in 1461. This battle led to a series of angry feuds, and a civil war broke out which came to be known as the Wars of the Roses. It was at the battle of Bosworth Field that Henry Tudor defeated Richard III in 1485. Shortly after, the two families became united by the marriage of Henry to Elizabeth of York and to honor this, the two emblems were joined, creating the Tudor Rose.

The Cabbage or Provence Rose is *Rosa Centifolia*. It is thought that it found its way to Europe from Turkey. It appealed greatly to the Dutch hybridizers of the 15th and 16th centuries, who were among the first to work extensively in breeding new roses, and they created many new varieties of Centifolia. The roses created by these hybridizers were unintentionally recorded for posterity in the works of the great Dutch Masters who portrayed the big, blowsy roses of pastel coloring on their canvases, often as decoration around well-proportioned ladies.

Right (above): Queen Elizabeth 1 was the last sovereign to reign under the symbol of the Tudor Rose.

Right (below): *Rosa centifolia* is well known as the 'Cabbage Rose' and was significant in the paintings of the Great Masters during the 15th and 16th centuries.

Left: 'Alba Maxima' is believed to be the 'White Rose of York,' the symbol of the House of York during the Wars of the Roses.

The Rose in China and Japan

The contribution of roses from China to the history of the rose is extremely significant. Tea roses and *R. rugosa* were featured in Chinese paintings and botanical drawings as long ago as the 10th century, but it is likely that they were grown there long before. Confucius, the great philosopher and teacher (551–479 BC), wrote that a large number of roses had been planted in the Imperial Gardens in Peking. It is interesting to note that during the Ming Dynasty, although roses were not considered as important as the peony or chrysanthemum, the growing of them and the production of rose water was only allowed if you were a member of the Emperor's family or a court official of high standing, and members of lower society could be sentenced to death if they were found to be cultivating roses.

We know that *Rosa laevigata* grew in the wild and it was included in the Herbal of Ch'iu Huang Peng Ts'ao in 1406. It was apparently shipped to Europe with other roses in the 1600s by the East India Company, who specialized in tea production. Soon after it was taken to America where it flourished and was given the name 'Cherokee Rose.'

One of the most important roses to be discovered in China was *Rosa chinensis*, a wild rose in varying shades of pink that flowered for most of the summer. It is believed that a variety of it, 'Parson's Pink' found it's way to the Île de Bourbon (now called Réunion) in the southern Indian Ocean where it was used for hedging along with the Damask rose, 'Quatre Saisons.' A natural hybrid occurred and was noticed in 1817 by the French Botanist Bréon, who collected seed, which he sent back to France where plants were raised and cultivated, producing the first Bourbon roses.

Also discovered in China, and probably as old as *Rosa chinensis*, were the Banksiae roses, a small group of rambling roses which are less than hardy but are completely thornless and very beautiful. Other species indigenous to China include *Rosa multiflora, R. rubus, R. indica odorata*, and *R. xanthina*. *Rosa indica odorata* was the first to reach Europe, sent from the Fa Tee Nurseries of Canton to Sir Abraham Hume in 1810, later it was to become better known as 'Hume's Blush.' The second was 'Park's Yellow Tea-scented China' named after John Parks, the collector who found it while on an expedition to gather plant material for the Royal Horticultural Society in 1824.

Some 21 years later in 1845, Robert Fortune discovered another yellow rose in a mandarin's garden. These two Chinese roses were responsible for the yellow coloring in some of the roses in existence today.

It is not known why the tea roses are so called, but it is said that it was because they were carried from China to Europe on the boats of tea-producing companies. Another theory is that their fragrance resembles that of the aroma of tea, but I cannot say that I find it so, unless of course the tea of the 1800s smelled very different from the tea of today. Tea roses became very fashionable with the Victorians, possibly because some of them were a challenge to grow. Hardy varieties would cope outside, but the more tender ones were kept in the conservatory or greenhouse, and they made excellent buttonholes, a popular adornment for Victorian gentlemen.

Japan too had several indigenous species, brought to Europe in a similar fashion to those discovered in China. We know from the collection of poems, *Manyoshu* or *Collection of a Thousand Leaves*, that roses existed there as early as the 8th century. Rose growing, as in China, was restricted to the upper classes and it was not until 1868, the beginning of the Meiji period, that it become more widespread. *Rosa multiflora* was the most prized and sought-after rose in Japan at this time, occurring in several forms which included 'Seven Sisters,' 'Watsoniana,' and 'Platyphylla,' all still with us today. *Rosa wichuraiana* was also popular, with a creeping habit and glossy leaves, it was named after Wichura in 1680 and brought to Europe in the 1870s, where it went on to be responsible for a large family of rambling roses. *Rosa rugosa* is another important species in the ancestral sense, discovered growing in Japan and brought to England in 1845, where it and its descendants are commonly used for hedging.

It is interesting to note that the Japanese are currently fascinated with the British tradition of growing roses and are prepared to pay handsomely for the flowers, especially old-fashioned ones. Indeed, Japan is one of the fastest growing markets for roses in the world.

The Empress Josephine

Josephine was as instrumental in the history of the rose as many of the outstanding hybridizers. Born in 1763 and baptized Marie-Josephe Rose Tascher de la Pagerie, she was the daughter of an impoverished nobleman. She married Vicomte de Beauharnais shortly after going to Paris at the age of 16, but he was later arrested and executed during the Reign of Terror. She bore two children to this man, a son who was to serve as a soldier under Napoleon Bonaparte and a daughter who was to marry Napoleon's brother, Louis, becoming Queen of Holland. Although she too was arrested, Josephine escaped the treatment of her late husband, and was released to repossess their dwelling and live once again in civil circumstances. Having met Napoleon at a ball in the Palais de Luxembourg, she married him in 1796. Napoleon did not like her given name, Marie-Joseph Rose, calling her simply Josephine instead.

In 1798, he purchased the Château de Malmaison, primarily for Josephine. Much of his time was spent there with her until his posting as First Consul in 1802. After this Josephine began collecting her famed treasures: wonderful works of art in the form of paintings and sculptures and beautiful jewelry, and it was also at this time that she turned her devotion to her garden. She employed British gardeners, among them the Scottish garden designer, Thomas Blaikie and Irishman John Kennedy.

Thanks to her husband's soldiers and with the assistance of scientists and diplomats, Josephine began bringing together rare and interesting plants from the world over, organizing them into the garden at Malmaison. The period of the Napoleonic Wars was a rich one for Josephine and her passion was well known, so much so that any captured vessels were thoroughly searched for any plants and seeds that they may have been carrying. Although the two countries were at war, John Kennedy was given a passport allowing him to openly pass over the British and French lines in search of new plants.

Through her endeavors to bring together as many rare and beautiful flowers as she could, Josephine discovered her passion for

Right: Redouté's paintings are accurate botanical works, giving us much information about the roses available during the time of Josephine. They are delightful to the eye, and have been used to embellish crockery and other domestic items.

Opposite: The Empress Josephine loved all that was material and built up a valuable collection of artifacts, but she also indulged in collecting for her garden and collated one of the best and most documented collections of roses from our past, a true addition to the heritage of our roses today.

roses and she instructed André Dupont to lay out a rose garden at Malmaison with no concern for expense. It was to become one of the largest and most beautiful of its time. Constantly striving to know more, Josephine made contact with every rosarian she could find in her neighboring countries, with French rose growers attending at her bidding. Her intention was to create a collection of every known rose, and she soon became well respected as an authority on the subject. Her collection was never complete and in pursing her passion to obtain every possible rose she created great competition among French nurserymen. Names such as Vibert, Laffay, Noisette, and Prévost, all French rose growers of the time are found in the old roses we grow today because of the outstanding

results of their hybridizing in competition to impress the Empress. Josephine's work and the desire of rose growers to impress her led to the rose being continually reinvented on a huge scale in France at that time, leaving the following generations a legacy of wonderfully beautiful roses.

At around this time, Pierre Joseph Redouté arrived in Paris from Belgium, where he was born in 1759, to work with one of his brothers as a scene painter in the

theater, where his work was noticed by the court painter Gerard van Spaendonck. Van Spaendonck was in charge of drawing flowers for the Jardin des Plantes, but preferred to work on commissions from other wealthy clients. He needed an artist he could trust to produce the plant records and so he employed Redouté.

From this start, Redouté worked as an illustrator for several botanists before being given the appointment as drawing-master to Queen Marie Antoinettte and then to Empress Josephine.

Napoleon purchased the Château de Malmaison for Josephine, but it was the garden that was to become her fascination.

At this point, and probably at the suggestion of the now divorced Josephine (she had been unable to provide Napoleon with any children), Redouté began to paint, rather than draw his subjects, unusually in watercolor (the most used medium of the time was gouache). His first works were of lilies, which he produced between 1802 and 1816, in all eight volumes and 468 plates. He dedicated this to Josephine, who had died in 1814 without seeing his work finished. In 1824 Redouté completed three volumes of *Les Roses*, consisting of some 167 color plates. This was followed by a further two editions,

the first with 160 plates and the second with 181. In each case the text was written by the botanist Thory. Although Redouté had Josephine's encouragement, it is interesting that he did not depend on her for the roses in his studies but was assisted in finding perfect specimens by the nurserymen of France.

Hugely acclaimed for his work, he had many pupils including royalty and members of the aristocracy, but in his later years Redouté was very hard up, having to paint to continue to survive. His "Choix des Roses" was produced at this time, but it is considered to be the least skillful of his works. He died while painting a lily on June 19, 1840. Although other botanical works have been created by artists, Redouté's must surely rank as the finest for their size, accuracy, and uniformity of style.

Thanks to Joephine's collection, which at her death had reached some 250 varieties, largely gallicas, and to Redoutés dedication to painting them, we have a superb record of the roses of the time, many of which are still with us today.

Sadly, after her death the

garden fell into decline. Her son, Eugéne, inherited Malmaison but he died in 1824 and his heirs soon sold it on. It then had a succession of owners and was badly damaged during the Franco-Prussian war of 1870. In January of the following year the siege of Paris saw the Château plundered and the gardens crushed. After this, little was done to restore Malmaison to its former glory. Out of respect for Josephine's work, Jules Gravereaux, an eminent rosarian of the time, began to collect together all the varieties of Malmasion in his own garden of L'Hay. He was successful in finding 197 of them. In 1912 he gave examples of these roses to Malmaison because the authorities had then decided to restore the Château and grounds.

Today the Château of Malmaison is a museum dedicated largely to Napoleon but with little of Josephine's other than some of her material treasures. The garden is under review and effort is being made to restore it but, I am told, with little success. The rose garden at Bagatelle and L'Hay, both containing collections made by Jules Gravereaux, are the places to see roses in Paris.

The Rose after Josephine

Josephine's influence was to continue. She had encouraged the breeders of her day, and those that followed were just as enthusiastic, producing many, perhaps not perfect but indisputably beautiful roses. The Victorians liked big blooms and many such varieties were introduced by them. In 1867, the first hybrid tea rose appeared: 'La France,' bred by Jean-Baptiste Guillot. The strains we have of this variety today are by no means healthy or strong, but one can imagine how the flower (which is large, mid-silvery pink, and perfumed) would have inspired the creation of what was to become one of the biggest groups of roses imaginable. The hybrid tea roses continued to appear at an ever-increasing pace alongside the hybrid perpetuals (and since the 1920s, the hybrid musks), except during the Second World War when very few roses were introduced. This is the date used by many rosarians as the division between old-fashioned and modern roses, although some still go back to 1865 and the introduction of 'La France.'

The popularity of the hybrid tea (often called the large-flowered rose today) and the other bedding-type rose, the floribunda (or cluster-flowered rose) continued

after the Second World War and for many more years, and they are still reasonably popular today, but perhaps are not used so much in the formal mass plantings favored in the 1950s and 60s. Today we are more likely to use this type of rose in mixed planting or in beds of mixed varieties.

Very much favored today are the modern shrub roses and the old-fashioned roses that Josephine adored, and we are also becoming more skillful in the use of climbers, ramblers, and the prostrate ground-cover roses. Miniature roses are less in demand but growers are becoming clever in their descriptions of new roses, finding that they can market them by giving them a name descriptive of their growth habit. Patio roses for example, while seeming to be a breed on their own, are termed so simply because they are small and neat, ideal subjects in pots on terraces patios and balconies. However, there are many other roses suited to this way of growing. Climbing miniatures are a group which, I suspect, would be happy tumbling over in the fountain-like manner found in many other roses but they were marketed as revolutionary. Likewise the ground-cover, or procumbent, roses which will happily climb if given support. Whatever new creations are ahead is not known, but whether perfection will ever be found is unlikely, for what is a perfect rose?

Rosa gallica officinalis is known as "The Red Rose of Lancaster" and also "the Apothecary's rose."

Using Roses

in the Garden

There has been a lot written about the design of rose gardens and the use of roses in new, mixed schemes or in established gardens. I aim here to amalgamate some of these already recognized ideas and to encourage you to look beyond the obvious; there are probably places in the garden that you had never before considered as being good spots for roses.

Traditional Supports for Climbers and Ramblers

There are many splendid ways of displaying climbers and ramblers on supports other than walls. Pillars and obelisks are the most obvious.

Usually around 8 ft. (2.5 m) in height, pillars can be a useful way of training roses in the smaller garden, as little width is required. They can be made of any durable material. Rustic poles are probably the most economical, but they can be much more formally structured, using

Right: Roses can be planted on one side of an arch and encouraged with training to grow over it, but if less of a one-sided look is to be achieved they should be situated on both sides.

Left: A structural feature is enhanced with roses beneath.

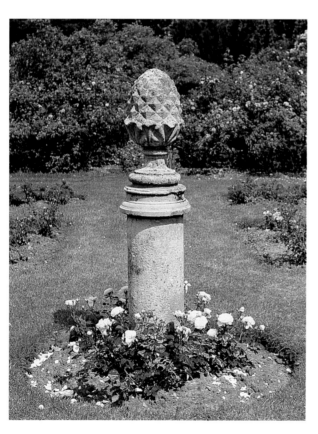

lengths of 4 x 4 in. (10 x 10 cm) timber, finished off with an elegant finnial (finnials can be purchased from good garden centers), and painted in your chosen color. Don't be afraid to experiment: the many different hues of roses allow for the adventurous use of color in the garden. Wrought-iron pillars and posts can also be purchased, but they can be expensive; there are much cheaper galvanized steel versions that come quite close to the real thing.

When growing a rose on a pillar, whether it is a climber or a rambler, try to wind the stems around the structure rather than just tying them in vertically. Flowering stems are produced from the leaf joints and the more the branches are trained to the horizontal, the more flowers will be encouraged.

Obelisks can have any number of sides but taper off to a central point. As with pillars, they are available in all manner of materials and styles. Simple, more rustic obelisks can be made from straight tree branches, but I would not endorse this on a large scale. Long thick canes or lengths of thin timber are a better alternative. It is a good idea to plant the rose first, then place the branches or canes around it in the ground at about

24 in. (60 cm) apart around the rose, bringing them together at the top where they can be tied with rafia or string. The rose can then be trained around the outer edge of the obelisk as it grows or, if using a shrub rose, encouraged to stay within the structure with the intention that only the flowers appear on the outer edges, but this can be difficult to achieve.

Arches act as doorways in the garden and if you have the space to create rooms or sections by planting long beds of climbing roses or other plants either side of them this works really effectively in forming "see-through walls." There are several ways of doing this. One is to position pillars at equal distances apart in a line on either side of the arch and to then place rope swags between each pillar; ramblers can then be trained up and then along to create garlands of flowers. If you prefer, the rope can be replaced by narrow sections of trellis. These are fixed between the tops of the pillars with another section lower down on which the roses can be trained, thus creating "windows" through the "wall." Or a series of arches can be positioned,

giving a selection of routes through which to pass. To create a denser barrier, create the screen with full panels of trellis to act as the supporting structure for roses or other climbing plants, with the arched doorway positioned somewhere along its length. If you do not have sufficient space, arches can be placed elsewhere, over a seat perhaps to create a bower, in front of doorways to sheds or other buildings, or over paths and gateways. Extra perspective can be created if a pathway leads to the arch, drawing the eye to it then beyond to some focal point, such as a statue, set farther back. A mirror, strategically placed beyond an archway, can create the illusion of space in the smaller garden.

A pergola is a series of connected archways adorned with roses or other climbing plants forming a tunnel, under which one can walk. In truth, this is a feature ideally suited for larger gardens, although it may be possible to position one over a pathway in smaller spaces. Pergolas can be made from anything

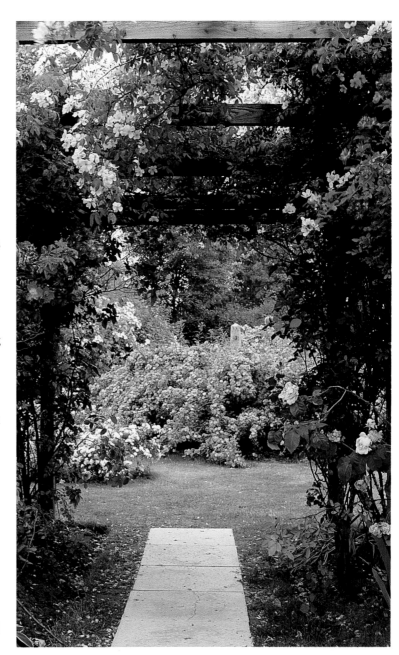

An archway or small pergola covered with roses frames the view to hidden gardens beyond.

strong enough to take the weight of many heavy blooms. The roses can be planted in a regular pattern with two of the same variety opposite one another forming bands of color along the length of the tunnel or less formally with mixed varieties. The choice is either to go for a mass show of color or to mix flowering times for a longer display but with

less impact; either way a cool shadowy tunnel will be the result. When erecting a pergola, bear in mind that it should be wide enough for two people to walk through side by side, and that it should be at least 8 ft. (2.5 m) tall to allow a few blooms to nod through unobtrusively.

The Use of Containers

Roses do not have to be grown in the ground, so why not try growing them in containers? The use of tubs and the like in the garden has two definite advantages. First, it provides the scope to be more adventurous with shape and color, and second, it makes roses portable so you can exchange one with another as the mood takes you.

There are all sorts of tubs and pots available to the gardener, but there are also more original items that can be used for this purpose. A wheelbarrow, for example, that has outlived its practical use can provide the ideal container, and a large one would accommodate two or three smaller roses. Its life can be extended by including a polythene liner, but do ensure there is good drainage

Use dead tree stumps as containers, with a little manipulation they are natural in appearance and ideal containers when treated correctly.

in the form of holes drilled in the bottom and a layer of pebbles below the compost. When the roses there have passed their best, simply wheel it to a less prominent position. Old tin buckets or even bathtubs can also be used in this way.

To make a plastic pot more interesting, make a few holes around the sides and plant a few low, spreading bedding plants or moss in them, or paint it. Bands of color can be effective, as can sponge

painting, there are also exterior textured paints available, but check on the label that they will coat plastic, it may be wise to rub a texture on to the pot with sand paper first. If you have a particular rose in mind, choose a paint color that will either compliment or contrast with the flowers.

You could also plant an old pair of large gardening shoes, with laces and tongue, with miniature roses, underplanted with a couple of bedding plants, take the laces out and pull the tongues forward to make room for the planting. Again add

Left:
Rambling
roses grown
through the
branches of
trees provide
color.

Below left:
Roses make
excellent
companions
to other
plants.

Below: The
gray foliage
of this com-
panion plant
is an excel-
lent foil for
the flowers
of this rose.

Roses in Mixed Beds and Borders

Roses are excellent companions to other plants if dotted in among them, and they can bring often overlooked qualities to the bed or border. They are chiefly sought after for their flower form and fragrance, but it should not be forgotten that there are varieties that produce hips and autumn foliage, and some with wonderful thorns, and some best grown for their attractive foliage. Many shrub roses are interesting structurally as they mature and can be used as specimen plants in mixed borders.

drainage holes to prevent waterlogging. Although they will not last forever they make an interesting feature on the doorstep and a conversation starter with callers.

If you have an unsightly tree stump in the garden, this too can be turned into a feature. Hollow it out, drill a few inconspicuous drainage hole through to the hollow, and plant a rose in it. The procumbent, trailing-type roses are effective when used in this way. To extend the life of the wood, the sides can be lined with polythene. Eventually the base of the trunk will rot and the roots will find their way down to the ground below.

If you have a dead tree, consider planting ramblers so that they climb through the branches but make sure the tree is safe first. Ramblers can also be grown against live trees, but they will need plenty of water and food in their

early years as the tree will use most of what is naturally available.

Trailing roses can be planted in large window boxes and miniatures in smaller ones. Hanging baskets also make useful containers and allow roses to be grown in a different way; again the trailing varieties are best in these but they should be positioned where thorny arching stems do not catch passersby.

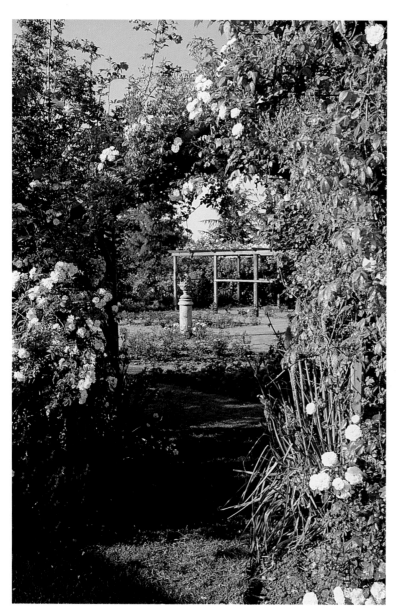

Through this archway the eye has immediate impact of flowers but is drawn to the garden beyond.

Where Roses Predominate

A garden that features a large number of roses can benefit from the addition of companion planting.

Edging beds and borders with perennials such as lavender or catnip, or small shrubs such as box that can be clipped to shape, finishes them off and prevents any low bare stems and weeds from showing. Include spring-flowering bulbs which although, not visible when the roses are flowering, will give color to the garden early in the year. Flowers of the shades of lavender, lilac, and purple compliment the majority of roses as well as do gray and silver-leaved plants. In recommending plants other than roses I am no expert, but the following are a few I like to see. The blue perennial sages supply both contrasting color and shape, as do delphiniums and foxgloves. Cornflowers and irises work well although some irises flower before roses. Scabious, in particular my favorite 'Clive Greaves' are very elegant, as are penstemons, which are available in a variety of colors are dense and low growing. Although not unlike roses in flower form, some of the peonies work very well with roses, as do poppies and low-growing hardy geraniums. For gray foliage try one of the ballotas, artemisias, or use stachys (lamb's ears) to cover the ground and deter weeds. Also look out for shrubs with purple foliage which lend themselves to the pastel shades of older roses, such as *Berberis thunbergii*. Buddlejas, in particular *B. davidii* (summer lilac) are quite large but will supply plumes of blue flowers, very attractive to butterflies, toward the back of a border. Mahonias, although spring flowering are evergreen and have very attractive leaves and hebes, even when not in flower, have dense evergreen growth. Clematis such as 'Lasurstern' or 'Jackmanii' and the blue wisterias can easily mingle with climbers and ramblers, and there are many perennials and shrubs with similar coloration that will lend themselves to shrub and bush roses.

Think of the shape plants assume and try to combine a variety among roses. The tall spears of the foxgloves, delphiniums, and astilbes contrast with the natural and graceful presentation of shrub roses, and underplanting bush roses with bubbly annuals, such as gypsophila and pansies not only provides another element but helps keep weeds down too. Think also of flower shape and size. There are very few roses with flowers smaller than 1 in. (2.5 cm) in diameter, so masses of dainty flowers in clusters will contrast with the larger rose blooms. When borne in clusters, the flowers of the rose form heads of an umbrella-like shape (called umbels or corymbs) usually nodding over slightly; try combining these with cluster-flowering plants of a different form, perhaps with racemes or panicles of flowers, such as wisteria or Russian vine.

Nothing but Roses

In a garden or border of roses alone, there are two ways of approaching the design. The first is to go for as much year-round color as possible, the second is to create a stunning en masse display for a shorter period. Both schemes have much merit and I dare not state a preference. In my own garden,

I want to enjoy roses for as long as possible but as a visitor to a garden, at the right time, I am captivated by masses of single-flowering roses, which are stunning to look at and have an overwhelming perfume. We all admire daffodils and rhododendrons when in bloom and appreciate them all the more because their beauty is fleeting, so why not with roses? I will leave this to personal preference.

The most practical answer could be a combination of both options. The short-lived beauty of the summer-flowering varieties will enhance the repeat-flowering roses at the time the garden is most lived in, while the season of interest is extended using earlier and later flowering, plus those with decorative hips and autumn foliage.

Using Roses in Garden Design

Whether starting from scratch, or simply adding the odd rose or two to an established garden, it is important to plan. Look through gardening books and rose catalogs to decide on the best roses for the situation, consult plant directories, such as the one in this book, and have a few alternatives in mind. Impulse buying is not a good idea, as there is such enormous diversity when it comes to roses that the chances are you will choose something totally unsuitable.

If a whole new rose garden is the intention, proper planning is essential. It is all too easy to plant too many or too few and very difficult to remedy this once the roses are *in situ*. As a rough guide I would suggest that shrub roses should be situated 3–4 ft. (1–1.2 m) apart, bush roses at roughly 18 in. (45 cm), and climbers at least 6 ft. (1.8 m) apart. However, these figures are only averages, and particularly in the case of the climbers may result in a dense covering.

If you are mixing shrub roses, remember to pay attention to their flowering period, mixing summer, repeat, and continuous flowering periods carefully to avoid bare patches later in the summer. Remember too the other features of the rose: hips, autumn coloring, leaf color, and decorative thorns.

Rose Hedges and Boundaries

Roses can make excellent hedges and dense, thorny protective barriers. The *Rugosas* are the prime candidates, with an extremely thorny disposition and strong, healthy foliage, many of them will produce big tomato like hips after flowering. You can also clip them with shears in spring to keep them in shape rather than pruning them individually. Other types of rose are suitable also, an assortment of species roses forms a truly delightful, naturally flowing boundary, while the taller floribunda roses will create a slimmer barrier.

Fences can be planted with rambling and climbing roses which, when trained out horizontally, will provide color from top to bottom. If you live in the countryside, however, be prepared to have them nibbled by deer, farm animals, or even squirrels.

Roses in the Wild Garden

Species roses are a useful addition to a wild garden. To create a native garden use *Rosa canina*, the Dog rose, or *R. arvensis*, the Field rose, both so commonly seen in our hedges. *Rosa pimpinellifolia* and *R. eglanteria* with its apple-scented foliage are also natives. Roses will attract insects, including bees and butterflies but don't forget that they also attract greenfly and caterpillars too.

Rosa arvenis also known as the 'Field Rose' is a native of Europe and is often found growing wild in hedges.

Selecting and

Purchasing Roses

Whether you are buying one rose for a particular spot, or many for a new rose garden, I would recommend that you do your homework first. There are so many to choose from, all with different qualities. Set your priorities: is perfume the most import factor, or is it flower color, or overall size and habit? Most specialized nurseries will have experts available to help you to choose, but their task will be difficult if you have no preconceived idea of what you are looking for.

Bear in mind where you are going to position your rose or roses. There are situations that would be unsuitable for most roses: in shade or on a cool, shady wall for example. There is a section toward the end of the Directory in this book which should aid in the selection of suitable varieties for such situations.

There are numerous books, such as this, on the subject of roses and a few encyclopaedias, all valuable in aiding selection, but growers' catalogs are also hugely helpful and there are some interesting sites on the internet. There can be no substitute, however, for seeing the roses in the flesh to help with your decision. Descriptions of color and perfume vary and conceptions of them differ; a rose considered scented by some may not be to others. There are many rose gardens to visit across the country and it should not be too difficult to find your nearest one from tourist information offices, or visit a rose nursery as, even

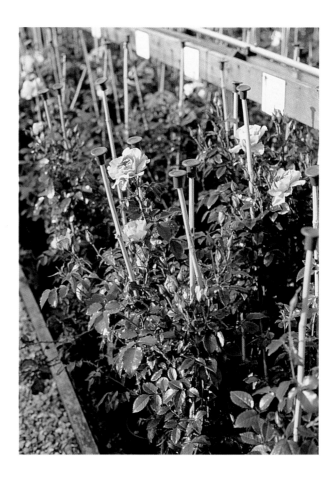

Right: Container roses are readily available during the summer months for instant purchases.

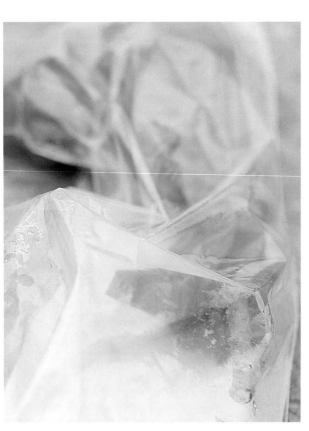

Left: Prepacked roses from outlets other than garden specialists are generally not good specimens. This one was purchased from a chainstore in June, at least two months after it should have been taken off the shelf. It had dried out, and there were tender young shoots struggling due to lack of water and nutrition.

if they do not have a garden as such they will often let you look at the roses in the field. There is an appendix of rose gardens to visit at the end of this book.

Flower shows are another good way of seeing roses and you can get good advice from the staff in attendance; even if you are not placing an order don't think that you are bothering them, that is why they are there. If the show is in early summer, such as the Chelsea Flower Show in London, the roses on display will have been forced under glass to achieve blooms and may be somewhat paler than they naturally would be, so check with the grower that they are a true representation.

Also take into account the way in which they are displayed. Some growers will take the trouble to create as garden-like an exhibit as possible, with the various types of rose displayed in the way they grow. Others, however, will cut the blooms and arrange them in bowls and vases; the onlooker then has no idea of the character of their growth.

There are three main ways that roses are bought. Specialized growers dealing in mail order will dispatch bare-rooted roses by mail or courier. Ordering can be done at any time, although the earlier an order is placed, the better both for availability and ensuring an early position in the line when the roses are sent. As they can only be dug up when they are dormant, roses will only be sent out at this time, usually between late autumn and early spring. While it is desirable, they do not have to be planted immediately, and can be left in their unopened package for a few days. If, after this time it is still not possible to plant them, they should be heeled in; this process is described in Chapter Four. Most growers will also allow you to collect your roses on a pre-determined date so they can have them lifted and packed ready for you.

If you are hoping to go along and purchase on the spot, it is wise to call the grower first. Plants cannot be manufactured to order, so it may be that the variety you are looking for is sold out. Some growers will have a selection already dug, but if not it may take some time for your particular roses to be made ready. The names and addresses of specialized growers can be found in the classified sections of gardening magazines where they frequently advertise.

Prepacked roses can be found almost anywhere in winter and spring and often later than this, from supermarkets to department stores. Buying roses in this form is far from

When planting a container rose in the summer, you must remember that it will need regular watering, especially in dry weather.

ideal. Packaging of polythene containing peat to keep roots moist encourages early growth and is a breeding ground for disease. Coupled with this predisposition is the fact that they have probably been stored at too high a temperature and will easily be damaged by low night temperatures and frosts when planted. If you must buy a rose in this way, take a good look at it through the package if you can. If there are young, yellowing leaf shoots and the roots or peat surrounding them appear to be dry, put it back on the shelf, this rose is unlikely to settle well in the garden.

It is sometimes possible

to obtain root-wrapped roses. These are a form of prepacked roses with only the roots enclosed in polythene. They are preferable to those discussed above as it is possible to study them better to determine quality and health. Look closely at the stems of the plant. If they appear at all wrinkled, it is likely that the plant has been allowed to dry out at some point, and this is not a good rose to buy.

Container roses are from the same crop as bare-rooted plants, but have been potted so that they can be bought and planted during the summer. They can be obtained from most specialized growers and garden centers but probably only on a cash

Check that
the rose you
are buying
has a good
structure
of strong
branches.

and carry basis, as they are
awkward and expensive to
transport. A specialist
would probably prefer to
sell you a bare-rooted plant
during the winter rather
than one that has been in a
pot since the previous year
or one that has been
recently potted. It is best to
leave a container rose in its
pot for a month if it has
been purchased early in the
summer, to allow the root
system to develop. If it is
removed from its pot too
early, the compost will not
have had a chance to settle
and will fall away, taking
with it delicate young

fibrous roots. If buying
from a garden center, it is
possible that the rose may
have been there for some
time. If you are able to
remove the pot, examine
the root system. Fine
strands of root showing
through the compost and
holding it together are
ideal. If there are many
thicker roots spiraling
themselves around the
inner shell of the pot, it
has become pot bound and
I would not buy it as it is
unlikely to transplant easily.

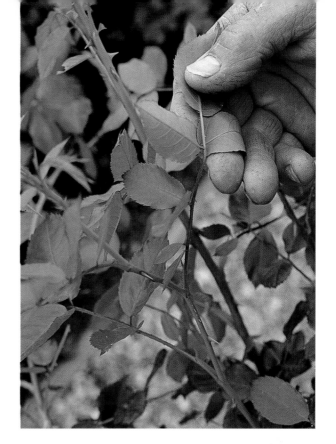

**Above right:
Try to avoid
buying plants
that show
signs of
disease on
their leaves.**

**Left:
A good
specimen will
have a well-
formed root
system and
several
strong
branches,
unlike the
plant in the
bottom pic-
ture, which is
spindly by
comparison.**

Choosing a good specimen

If roses are coming to you via the mail or courier, it will not be possible to choose your own plants, but reputable companies operating a mail-order service will have their reputation in mind and will grade the plants in the field to avoid dispatching poor quality examples. The same applies if you are collecting a preplaced order, as the roses will have been dug and packaged before your arrival at the nursery. If, when you unpack them you are dissatisfied with the quality of one or more of them, contact the supplier right away rather than planting the rose and hoping for the best. It may be that it will turn into an excellent plant after pruning, and many do, but your case will be stronger if you report your dissatisfaction early on. Good nurseries guarantee their roses and will honor this by replacing failed roses; although you may have to wait until the following season before receiving the replacement plant if a suitable plant is unavailable or if it died at the wrong time of year.

A good bare-rooted plant will have well-spread strong roots and at least three strong branches, although some rarer varieties, especially tea roses and china roses may have less, and this should be expected if they are your choice. It should arrive damp, having been well soaked before dispatch and stems should not appear wrinkled or damaged in any way.

Obviously it is impossible to look at the roots of a container rose other than to determine whether or not it is potbound, but if it is growing well, it can be assumed that all is well. As with the bare-rooted rose, there should be an even arrangement of at least three strong stems that are not damaged. Check that there are no signs of disease and that the compost is moist. Above all, ensure that the plant is labeled, as there is nothing more annoying than getting a plant home and realizing you've forgotten its name.

A year in the life of roses

So you've chosen your roses. The calendar of events following will give you some idea of what to expect from them and what you should do both with them (and already established plants) but, if you don't follow this exactly do not be too concerned; very few gardeners do but still get good results. The most important areas are all associated with young plants: if you get it right to begin with you are more than half the way to good roses. For precise details on all the aspects of rose cultivation you should refer to the following chapters, this acts merely as a breakdown of events.

Mid-winter
Bare-rooted roses are available now. If you haven't already ordered or received them (they have been leaving the growers since late autumn) order them now. Certain varieties may have long since become unavailable but many are still obtainable. Bare-rooted roses can be planted until early spring so you still have time but growers send out orders in the same rotation as they receive them, so you should act now or you will be last on the list.

Other than planting, there is little else going on in mid-winter, unless you were severely hit with a disease in the previous season, in which case a wash with a fungicide may be appropriate. Take advice from your local garden center or grower as to which to use, but ensure that you wash both the rose and the surrounding soil and, if appropriate, any support on which roses are growing. Spores from wind-spread diseases can winter over in the soil or on dead leaves close by to re-emerge the following year.

When planting a bare-root rose it is a good idea to shake the plant when half the soil has been returned to the hole to ensure that there are no pockets of air left.

Late winter
Any winter activities can take place in late winter, and this may be the last month to complete them successfully as roses can begin to grow in early spring. The time for pruning is late winter and early spring, after the worst frosts are over. If you wish to transplant a rose from one part of the garden to another this is the last opportunity; doing so in early spring is more risky, as the ground will be beginning to warm up and roots starting to grow. Roses in pots and tubs that have been in there for two years or more should have some of their compost removed and replaced with new compost.

Early spring
Finish pruning early in the month and top dress with proprietary rose food. This month is the last opportunity for planting bare-rooted roses, before the weather warms up. As the leaves begin to show, start a spraying regime if you intend to use chemicals, and repeat every ten to fourteen days.

Mid-spring

Mid- and late spring are probably the least busy times of the year as far as the growing of roses is concerned. Flowers are not yet developed and disease is at a minimum; although you should keep up a spraying or organic regime to prevent it taking control. As the weather warms up, start to water new roses regularly, especially if they are in pots.

Late spring

Ramblers and vigorous climbers should now be producing growth. It is worth taking the trouble to tie them against their supports in the direction you want them to grow, as the wood will be soft and pliable at this stage, and it will prevent them from becoming accustomed to growing in the wrong fashion. This will need to be repeated throughout the summer if you are to remain in control of rampant varieties. If you are trying your hand at breeding you can start now on roses under glass.

Early summer

Tasks in the garden are increasing in number and this is particularly true when it comes to roses, but the beautiful flowers and perfumes act as inspi-

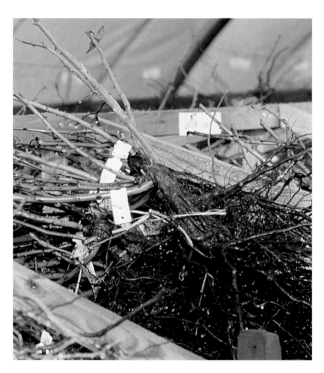

Above: Bare root roses ready for the nurseryman to dispatch to the customer.

Left: Spent rose blooms should be removed in order to encourage further production of blooms.

ration. Watering of new roses will need to be done frequently, unless it is a particularly wet summer. Flowers that have died will now need to be removed and extra care must be taken to keep pests and diseases at bay. It is now, as the more established roses are blooming, that you will notice proliferation, and suckers may be emerging from under the soil, these should be removed as early as possible. Hybridizing can take place out of doors now and in commercial rose growing, this is the month when budding often starts. Cuttings can be taken now but they will need more looking after than if you wait for early autumn. Keep tying in climbers and ramblers.

Midsummer

Roses are still blooming well but many will be going over. All varieties that flower repeatedly or continuously should be deadheaded to encourage the next flush, as should once-flowering ones unless they set hips. Apply a second application of rose food to support growth into the autumn. Chemical or organic pest and disease control should still be ongoing, as should watering of young and potted plants. Remove any recently developed suckers and any leaves that have become diseased.

Late summer

Late summer can be a bad time for disease so try to keep on top of it, both in precautionary control and in the removal of diseased leaves. Other than this, there is little of excitement happening. Keep up the watering and training of climbers and ramblers, although their growth will have slowed down now.

Early autumn

Many roses will have stopped producing large numbers of blooms, perhaps an odd one here or there, but a few will be blooming well at this time. Remontant shrub roses can look quite unkempt by now and can be tidied up. Howver, leave the once-flowering varieties or you will remove next year's flowering growth. Keep up pest and disease control and watering. Hips are now fully formed and some roses will be showing signs of magnificent autumn color.

Mid-autumn

Roses are now beginning to slow down and ready for their dormant period. Slow down the watering, but it is still a good idea to control disease. Hardwood cuttings can now be taken and thought given to the transplanting of mature roses, although this should not be done until the plant is fully dormant. Rake up fallen leaves and destroy them, as they may be harboring unwanted disease spores. This is a good time to make preparation for any bare-rooted roses you may have ordered, by improving the soil and digging the holes.

Opposite: Hips of *Rosa Pimpinellifoli.* The flower is mahogany brown in color.

Right: A few varieties of rose suffer from viruses which are not contagious to other roses but are often represented by miscolored leaves.

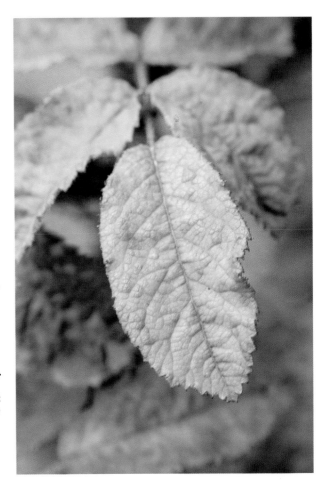

Late autumn

Bare-rooted roses are now available. In this month we see the arrival of the dormant season, and the activity going on now can be done at any time until early to mid-spring. Roses can be moved in the garden if it is felt necessary and winter washes can be applied to prevent spores of diseases such as rust and blackspot from wintering over. Put up protection around tender varieties to keep the frosts that are soon likely to arrive from damaging or killing them.

Early winter

Early winter is as late autumn, except that the risk of frost is increasing, so it is a good idea to check that the protection you have put in place for less tender varieties is still secure.

Planting and

Pruning Roses

Soil Improvement

Giving a rose the right start in the garden is probably the most important thing you will ever do for it, which is why preparation and planting procedure are so important. Roses enjoy a slightly acid to neutral soil, one with a pH of about 6.5, but they will tolerate a degree of alkalinity and will not show signs of being unhappy in soils of up to pH 7.5. If you are in doubt as to the levels of acidity or alkalinity in your soil, testing kits are readily available from garden centers and are easy to use. As a rule of thumb (except for city dwellers), if there are dog roses growing in hedges or wild nearby, your soil is likely to be suitable for roses.

If you do find that your soil is too alkaline, it can be improved with the addition of some well rotted cow manure, peat will do the same but it is a finite resource and should therefore be used sparingly. Garden compost is usually quite acidic but ensure that it is well rotted.

Even if your soil is not alkaline, it will still benefit from the addition of organic matter which will improve the structure of the soil as well as adding to its nutritional value. Organic matter will also help maintain moisture in free-draining soil as well as help improve heavy, water-retaining clay.

Conversely if your garden is too acidic the addition of powdered lime will help. Much is said about the use of chemical fertilizers in the soil, but opinions constantly change, just as they do regarding human nutrition. Some believe that they reduce resistance to disease, in particular to rust, but I have yet to experiment. What is certain is that in an increasingly urban world, the freedom to obtain natural nutrient is decreasing and occasionally soils need a pick-me-up; if the use of chemical fertilizers is not overdone I cannot help but feel that they are appropriate. What is even more important is that plants receive a balanced diet of nutrients. We cannot be sure that this is the case when using organic matter but the man-made alternatives are carefully mixed to ensure that this is the case.

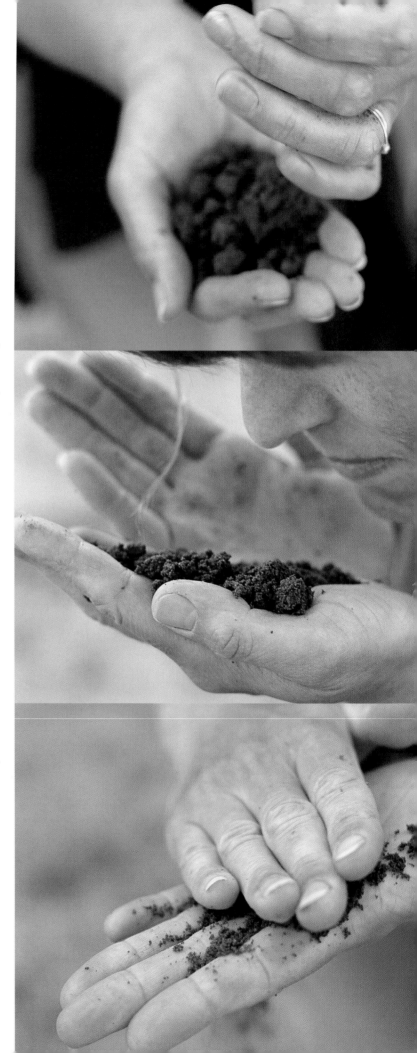

Whatever the makeup of your soil, it will benefit from good old-fashioned double digging before it is planted. This may not be possible if you are adding roses to existing planted areas but if you are starting from scratch it will both aerate the soil, making root penetration easier, and bury surface weeds and weed seeds. To double dig an area, first remove a trench of soil, a spit (spade depth) deep leaving it in the wheel barrow or on a tarpaulin laid across the ground and fork over the bottom of the trench. Then dig another trench adjacent to the first, returning the soil to the first trench, again forking the bottom of the new trench. Continue to do this until you have an empty, forked trench at the end and fill this with the soil taken from the first trench. If you do this in autumn but do not intend to plant until early the following year, you will be able to leave the clods of earth solid, as winter frosts will brake them up and a fine tilth will be easier to create nearer planting time.

If, however, you plan to plant close to the time of digging, it will be necessary to create a finer tilth at the same time.

If your soil is very heavy it may need additional drainage and this can be done at the same time as double digging. Roses hate being dry but will not thrive in waterlogged ground either. There are several ways of doing this. If you are planting in isolated positions, rather than a quantity of roses together in a bed or border, the easiest solution is to dig the hole to twice the necessary depth and lay some gravel in the base. For the rose bed or border, however, it is worth laying more sophisticated drainage in the form of plastic piping, although you could repeat the gravel application at regular intervals.

Opposite: Soil can be improved with the addition of man-made or garden composts, well rotted cow manure, and fertilizers. It is wise to check the pH of the soil before using additives to keep the balance around neutral.

Specific Replant Disease

Roses should not be planted in places from where other roses have been recently removed, for the soil will be "rose sick." It is believed that roses leave certain chemical secretions in the soil which are offensive to other roses. The new ones will grow poorly, often suffering from die-back and will be very prone to disease.

There are a few ways of approaching this problem. The first is to plant the area with some other plants, giving the chemicals time to leach away, but this should be for a minimum of two years. The most obvious instant solution is to interchange the problem soil with some from another "clean" area of the garden, but this is clearly not practical if you are replanting an entire bed or border; this is where the use of chemicals comes in. There are sterilants available that in certain dilution claim to rid the soil of rose sickness and by and large they are quite good. You cannot replant immediately but you do not have to wait too long. The alternative is to employ professionals to sterilize the soil using gas pumped under polythene, but this is only economical on a large scale, for municipal plantings or other large gardens open to the public, and not necessary in the average home garden.

Rose sickness is the reason why commercial growers rotate their crop using different fields in separate years, leaving some dormant, or leasing them to farmers who will grow something entirely different.

Planting Roses

The rose you are dealing with will either have bare roots or be in a pot. At the end of the day the results will be much the same, but there are fundamental differences in the way they are planted, so I deal with them separately.

Planting Bare-Rooted Roses

Before you plant a rose you need to identify the union. This is the gnarled area between the roots and the branches; it is the place where the rose was originally budded, and you will probably be able to see where the top of the root stock was cut off. The hole you dig should be deep enough that the union is about 1 in. (2.5 cm) below soil level to deter suckers. Some of the older shrub and climbing roses may even develop their own roots from the area of stem below the ground. The hole should also be wider than the breadth of the plant's roots, when they are spread. This will ensure future stability because the roots will be encouraged to grow in all directions through less compacted earth.

Now you have dug your hole it is a good idea to break up the soil in its base a little with a fork, to assist root penetration, and mix a handful of bonemeal into it. Cast another handful of bonemeal over the soil that will be put back in the hole and mix this in also.

Now position the rose in the hole, spreading the roots out, and holding the plant upright. Add some of the soil so that it stands freely on its own, then return about half the soil. Shake the roots at this stage to avoid pockets of air being trapped, and firm gently with a foot before returning the remainder of the soil. Once again firm with the feet before tidying the surface soil and labeling. If planting took place in late autumn or early winter, it is wise to check the stability of the rose plant a couple of times before it starts to grow in spring. No fibrous roots will have been produced to anchor it in position, and the wind may have caused it to rock a little. Once it does start to grow it will require regular watering

The hole should be wide enough to accommodate the roots which will be spread out and deep enough to cover the base of all the stems.

1

2

1. Add stones to the base of the pot to aid drainage.

2. Ensure that the rose can be placed deep enough to cover the base of the stems. If it is too deep add a little more compost to the bottom of the pot.

3. Leave around an inch between the level of the compost and the edge of the pot, to prevent compost running away as the plant is watered.

Planting Containerized Roses

To ensure that the compost is moist before planting, it is wise to soak the pot in a bucket of water, or similarly sized vessel. As with bare-rooted roses, the hole you dig should be wider than the pot and deep enough to cover the union. It is quite likely that the nurseryman will have left the union showing as rose roots are often difficult to fit in a pot (roses are not actually grown in pots but containerized at around 18 months old). Fork the base of the hole, mix in a handful of bonemeal, and another into the heap of soil waiting to be returned to the hole.

When removing the rose from its pot, try not to disturb the ball of compost surrounding the roots as this will cause the young fibrous roots to be broken. In the days of polythene pots this was easily achieved by slitting the polythene with a knife, but it is more difficult with a rigid pot. Don't grasp the base of the rose to pull it out as this too could disturb the roots, instead turn the pot upside down and tap its edge against the edge of a work-bench or table top. If it resists, squeeze around the sides of the pot gently and then have another go. Once it is successfully removed, place it in the hole, and position so that it is upright; sometimes roses are not upright in their container because the size and nature of their roots dictated that they could not be. Carefully fill the gap around the rootball with soil, firming gently.

Standard Roses

It is very important that standard roses are well staked and that the stake is positioned before planting takes place. First, dig the hole so that, in the case of a bare-rooted standard, the roots can be well spread, and so that the mark on the stem, showing its previous planting depth, is well below soil level to allow for settlement. A containerized standard should be planted in a hole that is deeper and broader than the pot for the same reasons. As with other roses, lightly fork the soil at the base of the hole and mix in a handful of bonemeal, both in the hole and in the heap of soil. The stake, which should have been treated with wood preservative can then be driven in to a depth of at least 18 in. (45 cm). It should be off-center and on the windward side and the right height to reach to just below the branches. To make it easy and less harmful to the rose when changing the stake in years to

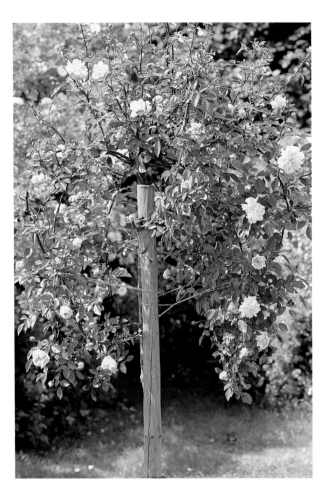

This weeping standard is well supported with a strong treated stake.

Moving Established Roses

Success in this endeavor will be determined by the age and size of the plant in question; a huge rambler will clearly be more problematic than a bush rose, and will have larger roots, making it difficult to dig up intact. You should only attempt to move roses in their dormant season, when they are not in leaf and will lose very little water. First, cut back the branches fairly hard, don't worry about exact pruning at this stage, it can be done later when there will undoubtedly be some dieback to remove. Now, if the rose is isolated enough, dig a trench as deep as possible around the rose, to give you ease of movement when it comes to digging below the roots, which is the next task. If the rose is large, this be a two-person job. As you dig, the plant should be gently pushed away from the side you are working on to give you access nearer the middle.

Once you have completed the removal, it can now be replanted in its new position, following the guidelines for other roses. Watering with a liquid seaweed extract before planting will encourage new root development. Don't forget that it will probably be very thirsty.

Planting a Rose Hedge

Rose hedges can be formal or informal. Informal hedges are best created from different varieties of roses combined for a natural combination of flower color, form, and overall growth habit, and therefore should be planted with this in mind. Formal hedges of one variety or a mixture of similar roses, such as rugosas, should be planted in a regimental fashion with the plants at an equal distance from each other. If a broad barrier is desired, two rows of the roses can be planted adjacent to each other but with the plants assuming a zigzag pattern, so as to create depth and fullness between plants.

come, a piece of drainpipe can be positioned in the soil at this time and the stake inserted into this. Position the standard against the stake and hold it there using one of the ties. Now start to in-fill and firm with the feet, or in the case of a containerized standard, if the hole is not much larger than the rootball with the handle of a garden tool or similar to fit the gap between the rootball and the side of the hole. The ties should be positioned at the top, bottom, and

center of the stem, unless it is a half standard when two should be enough. Use spacers to prevent the roses from coming into contact with the stake and loosely tighten. Remember to check them after about a month, as ground settlement may have caused them to move.

A mulch can be of compost or more refined bark or small pebbles.

To Mulch or Not to Mulch

A mulch is a layer of material, either organic or non-organic, designed to retain moisture in the soil and suppress weeds. The effectiveness of it rather depends on the material chosen. Black plastic sheeting or the modern polypropylene version are probably the most successful of all, but do you really want them spoiling the appearance of the garden? I would only advocate their use if the roses are of procumbent nature, so that will eventually hide the ugliness of the material. Used under such roses, this type of sheeting will suppress weeds until such time as it breaks up, which is useful as it is most awkward to weed through procumbent roses. There are several other possible options when it comes to choosing a mulch. Bark chippings are quite good, but in time they will blow away or disintegrate, providing good organic matter but no mulch. Coconut shells are also a possibility and are fine so long as you can put up with a chocolate aroma pervading the garden. Some use grass cuttings, but they are very high in nitrogen and will encourage fewer flowers and much young growth, which will be more susceptible to disease. Probably the most successful, unobtrusive mulch is shingle.

In time weeds will get through, but it will cool the soil and not blow away. There are several different types available, but the choice will be dependant on personal taste and the style of the garden.

Pruning and Training

Why prune roses you may ask? The answer is simple. It prevents plants from becoming top heavy, rejuvenates growth so that more flowers are created, and helps eliminate disease by removing older growth that has previously suffered and may be harboring wintered-over disease spores. Pruning, coupled with training where necessary, also gives the gardener the chance to become a designer in some small way, especially with climbing, rambling, and larger shrub roses; they will never be ideal subjects for topiary but they are controllable. Pruning a rose should not be seen as a sadistic procedure, but should be viewed more like a hair-cut for the benefit of the plant.

Pruning is not the difficult assignment suggested by some, although it can be time consuming if you have several roses, but rewarding also. You do not need many tools: a good sharp pair of clippers, long-handled pruning shears for thick or high branches, and a thick pair of gloves. Scissors, especially those used by florists, are useful for daintier candidates, such as miniatures.

Check ties to prevent them from becoming too tight as the plant grows and branches thicken. The wire on this branch has caused damage that will attract infection.

When pruning, always consider the following points. Wood that has become damaged in some way, by rubbing against other branches, or being snapped in the wind, and swollen areas around old ties should be removed as areas such as these provide ideal entry for disease. When two branches are touching but are not yet damaged it is a good idea to remove one before they begin to chaff each other and any diseased growth should also be cut away. Try, where possible, to make cuts at an angle, above and slanting away from a bud and bear in mind which direction that bud is facing; you do not want new branches to grow toward the center of the plant. Shrub and bush roses should be kept open, if possible, by removing central tangled growth and climbers should either be well tied in against their support or pruned with shape in mind.

Train climbers and ramblers in as many outward directions as possible to encourage lateral growth.

Pruning Newly Introduced Roses

Before looking at the methods employed in annual rose pruning, it is important to understand the necessity and benefit of hard pruning a newly purchased bare-rooted rose. Whatever the type of rose in question, its branches should be heavily reduced in size; bush or shrub roses to around 6 in. (15 cm) in length and climbers and ramblers to about 10 in. (25 cm). If you do not do this, the outcome will be top-heavy plants with sparse and bare branches at the base. It is very difficult to encourage low growth later on in the plant's life so, at its first introduction to the garden, it must be dealt with harshly. I myself have fallen victim, it is so easy to give priority to the desire of enjoying early and previously unknown

flowers over the shape and performance of the plant, in several instances I have had to underplant with perennials to disguise the leggy results of my neglect. Roses purchased in containers do not require any pruning until the correct season arrives, as the grower will have already given them the necessary treatment at the time of potting them.

It is also worth checking the "snag" at planting time. This is the area of the plant at which the branches of the understock were cut away from the roots once the implanted bud had been accepted in the process of commercial production. It is noticeable as a protrusion from the union (the area between the roots and branches), which looks like a branch that has previously been well pruned, in other words a stump. It should be reduced in size so that it is flush, if possible, with the union. If it is left protruding it is possible that it will, in turn, produce fresh branches of the understock which, as they are technically suckers, are likely to be more vigorous than the budded cultivar. In this scenario they will prove themselves stronger, depriving the upper part of the plant of nutrient, and eventually taking over.

If you have purchased your bare-rooted rose direct from a reputable nursery, the snag will have undoubtedly been removed. Wholesale companies and, in turn, their outlets may be less concerned with such detail.

Ramblers

Rambling roses, by and large, flower on the growth they make in the preceding season and this is usually, although not always, in the form of long arching canes. These grow with much vigor from the base of the plant, although on occasion similar new growth will form higher up. In their first year or two, assuming they were hard-pruned on arrival if they were bare-rooted plants, it is best to give them their freedom to establish and form a good root system and begin to flower (ramblers will often take up to three years to produce blooms). Thereafter a pruning regime can be established. They should be pruned in late summer after flowering; it is foolish to allow them to expend nutrients on branches that have already flowered unless, of course, they bear hips, in which case pruning should be left until early spring. Canes can be trimmed to any length and will still be flower productive, but if they are all removed completely your rambler will be devoid of bloom.

There are two ways of pruning a rambler, entirely dependant on the manner in which you wish it to grow. When trained out horizontally, on a fence for example, the plant will withstand the removal of all growth that has previously flowered, the new canes can then be trained to form the overall structure. To achieve this you will need to remove the ties holding it in place, allowing it to fall away toward the ground. Work can then commence and once completed, or during pruning, the selected remaining growth can be re-attached. Encourage them as they grow, with regular tying in, into a fan shape or outward in both directions. This keeps the plant young and thin while encouraging new growth but is not always practical, especially if the purpose of growing the rambler is to disguise an eyesore. If you want a more permanent although deciduous disguise, be less severe in pruning, removing only the older wood, but still be hard on the odd branch or two to keep some young growth lower down. Some ramblers are best left unpruned, especially those climbing through the branches of trees or those sprawling on a bank; their position may make it impossible anyway. Most ramblers will be happy if never pruned or if they are left unpruned for three or four years, especially the most vigorous tree climbers, but to encourage rejuvenation a good hard prune now and then will work wonders.

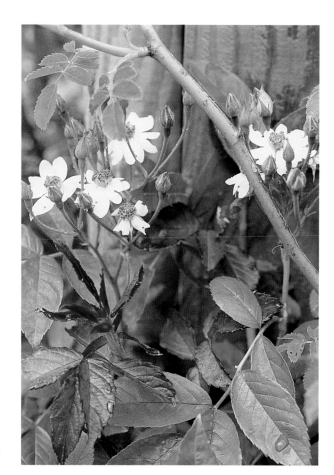

Right: Light pruning during the growing season will encourage new flowering growth as well as keeping the plant tidy.

Below: A hard-pruned rambler will produce strong new growth from the base.

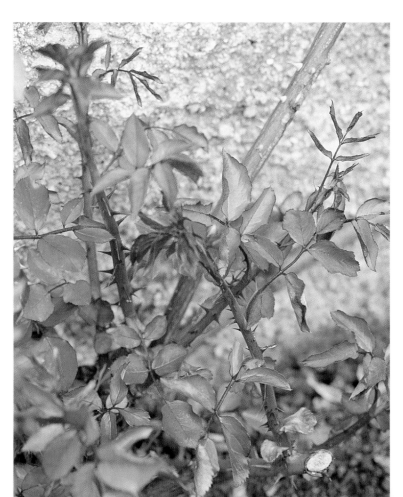

Climbers

Climbers flower on current season's growth and are therefore treated a little differently. They will send out strong climbing stems, but these are usually slower growing than those of the ramblers. As young plants, they should be trained outward as much as possible and fixed to the trellis or the support you have in place. From these branches will grow the 'lateral' stems that produce the flowers. With age, climbing stems will appear higher up, and these too should be spread outward to encourage flowering.

When pruning, reduce the lateral stems to about a third of their length, and they will produce flowering stems the next summer, which are then treated in the same way, and so on in future years.

As with all roses, but most importantly with climbers, watch out for rubbing stems. Their growth and the training method applied to these roses is such that stems are very likely to come into contact. Rubbing stems will soon become chaffed, such damaged areas will provide ideal conditions for disease to enter.

Once-Flowering Shrub Roses

Included here are the gallicas, centifolias, mosses, albas, and damasks as well as the diverse species roses. Other than when growth is untidy, it is often best to leave these unpruned. If they need a trim, it is best done in summer just after they have flowered, enabling them to make more flowering growth before the frosts for the following year. Don't prune varieties that set hips unless you have to, as autumn hips are a great source of pleasure at a time when there is less interest in the garden.

If you do prune, concentrate on areas of weak and damaged wood, or leggy dense growth that may make the rose look top heavy. Above all, try not to spoil the character of the plant or be too harsh in your treatment; severe pruning is best done in the dormant season, when there will be less water loss, although it will reduce the flowering potential for that year.

Repeat-Flowering Shrub Roses

Pruning roses from this group will benefit both their shape and flowering capabilities. Thin out the plant if it is becoming too dense, remove thin growth that is unlikely to produce or support heavy flowers, and remove any damaged growth. When this is done, the main stems can be reduced to different levels, some by about one-third of their length, from which earlier flowers will appear and some by about two-thirds, from which new growth will be encouraged lower down and will be of benefit to the plant in future seasons. The following year, taller branches can be treated to a low prune, and those cut hardest the previous year can be left taller, thereby creating a rotation of younger growth. Summer pruning can be done, if necessary, when deadheading, but this should be a light trim for the benefit of appearance rather than a full-scale prune. If you have a variety that produces hips, deadhead the early flowers, but leave the later ones untouched, otherwise you will obviously loose the hips.

Above: This shrub rose has become untidy and has many crossed stems which will start to rub against each other if some are not removed.

Right: The shape is now improved and the effect of the pruning will be that more growth is produced lower down on the branches that remain.

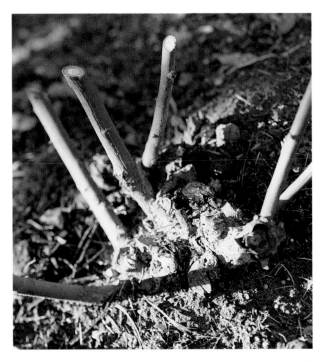

Standard Roses

Standard roses come in three forms, and are simply a bush, shrub, or climbing/rambling rose budded on to a host stem, therefore it follows that the pruning and training principle are much the same as for that cultivar not grown as a standard, so I refer you back to earlier text. The exception to this is the weeping standard because the desired effect is for the branches to cascade down, not grow up against a support in the way ramblers and climbers are encouraged to. There are three ways of doing this. The first is to purchase a trainer, this is an umbrella-shaped, wire frame, rather like an upturned hanging basket. This is attached to the top of the stake, (which has to be taller than the standard stem) and fits over the branches. The theory is that the leaves and flowers will grow densely enough to disguise it, but it is visible for quite some time and, I think, positively ugly. The second method is to attach a wire hoop to two or three stakes surrounding the standard and to tie the branches to it but again I find this unsightly, although it can be removed once the branches are heavy enough to remain there on their own. The best method by far, in my opinion is to draw the branches in, by securing them with a length of soft string with one end tied to the stake. The string is largely hidden by the branches and the whole effect far less contrived. Whichever method is employed,

Left: Hybrid teas and floribundas should be hard pruned each year to prevent them becoming top heavy.

Below: To encourage the branches of a weeping to fall, tie them toward the stake. As the branches grow, the string will be hidden.

Pruning Bush Roses

Bush roses are candidates for hard pruning, especially in their first year. The principle is to keep growth low, as they quickly become leggy and top heavy if not dealt with regularly, and to maintain an open well shaped plant. Thin, bendy stems are unlikely to produce good flowers, so these should be pruned the most, leaving the stronger branches to form the shape and character of the plant. Try to cut above an outward-facing bud to prevent overcrowding in the center of the plant and remove any dead or diseased wood. When removing branches at their base, make the cut as low down as possible, as after several years of this treatment the plant will look most unsightly if there are lots of dead stumps here. In the autumn, after flowering, trim bush roses back a little, both to tidy them and make them less prone to rocking in mighty winter winds.

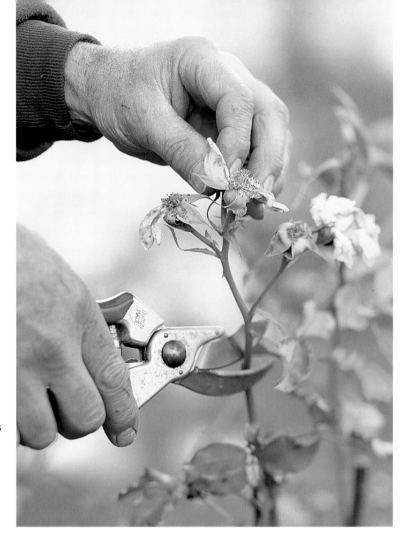

it is important to create a balance of branches cascading equally on all sides. It is usual for the standard to have been budded in three places equidistant around the stem to guarantee an even distribution of branches but, on occasion, the plant may have only received two buds, in which case more care must be taken during the process of training. While I would not advocate the purchase of a standard rose that has received only one bud, experienced rose gardeners will have no trouble in training such a plant given time.

When you are pruning or training a standard rose, check the ties that hold the stem to the stake, ensure that they are not perishing or too tight, but also look for signs that they might be chaffing the stem, in which case they are too loose. A standard should be supported by at least two ties, in the case of a weeping standard three, if there are less you need to add to them.

Hedges and Procumbent Roses

Because there are a lot of twiggy branches on a hedge or in a large bed of low-growing, procumbent roses they can be treated in a more general fashion, rather than by tackling one branch at a time. They will even respond to being trimmed with an electric or gas-powered hedge trimmer, but do be careful if lots of thorny pieces of stem start flying through the air; always wear protective eye goggles. Many rose hedges are of rugosa roses which have wonderful autumn foliage and hips, but if you desire a neat and tidy perimeter finish, you will need to prune the plants so that they are narrower at the top than they are at the base. More vigorous growth will appear higher up on the plant and by the time they come into flower the width will be constant. Prune the hedge to the height of the shortest plant for an even finish.

Clusters of flowers should be removed just above a lower leaf joint.

Deadheading

Deadheading is simply speeding up nature's process of dealing with dead flowers. When a flower goes over it, along with the uppermost part of the stem (all that is above the first leaf joint) will die and fall to the ground, unless the variety sets hips.

There are two ways of dead-heading roses: one is tried and trusted, the other is relatively new and, for my part, untried. To carry out the first method, select a leaf joint below the dead flower that is facing outward, and cut away all above this joint. The bud, hidden under the leaf stalk will then grow and produce flowers. The advantage of dead-heading in this way is that you can control the shape of the plant a little during the summer, as well as the winter. The new method does not carry with it this possibility as less growth is removed: it involves snapping off the flowerhead at the abscission layer, which is recognizable as a slight bulge on the stem usually at the first leaf joint. It is said that the more foliage a plant has the better its performance, and also that the rose will produce its next flush more quickly and with larger numbers of blooms. I shall be trying this method at the earliest opportunity.

Suckers

Throughout the growing season, suckers may well appear from the roots. If the plant is commercially produced by budding, these fleshy stems will be from the rootstock and are therefore not of the budded cultivar that appears above the ground. If the plant has been there a while, or if it were produced from a cutting, in other words if it is on its own roots, then the sucker need not be removed as it is part of the cultivar. To know the difference can be difficult, and it is an old wives' tale that suckers have seven leaves on a leaflet and cultivated roses five, this applies to some, but not all modern bush roses; many shrub roses, ramblers and climbers have seven. If you know that the rose was originally budded, the best way to determine whether or not the stem is a sucker is to trace it back to its place of origin, removing some of the soil around it to see what you are doing. If it originates from the root or low on the union (the barked area between the branches and roots) it is a sucker and should be removed, if it coming from above this area it should be left. If you are still unsure, compare the leaves and thorns with similarly aged parts of the rose itself. Are the leaves the

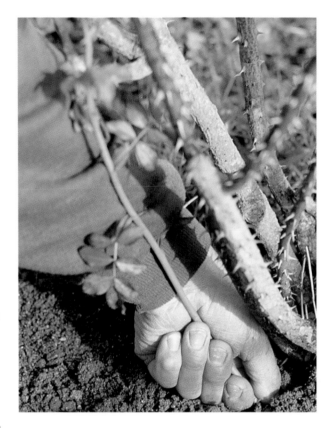

Right: When removing a sucker try to trace it back to its origin and remove it carefully and cleanly.

Left: Shoots that appear on the stem of a standard rose are suckers and should be removed as cleanly as possible.

same shape and color? How many thorns are there and how are they shaped? Is the growth of equal vigor? Try a second opinion. Suckers should be removed as soon as they are noticed, before they sap too much energy from the rest of the rose. If left, they will be seen to be much more vigorous than the cultivated plant and will gradually dominate until they take over.

You should trace a sucker back to its point of origin, placing the thumb between it and the root and forcing it away by pushing down. The tear should be as clean as possible to prevent it from re-shooting. Rose gardeners in days gone by had an instrument designed specifically for this, called a "spud," a long-handled tool intended to sit over the base of the sucker, and when pressure was applied it simply tore it away. If the sucker is the same as the plant itself, you may be able to remove it with some root attached. You then have another plant for elsewhere in the garden or as a gift to a fellow gardener, this is discussed in more detail in the following chapter.

Propagation

There are various ways of propagating roses; some require more skill than others but most can be done on a small scale in the garden with great success.

Budding

This is the method most commonly used by commercial rose growers as it uses small amounts of propagation material, has a high success rate, and produces strong, salable plants. The actual process of budding calls for dexterity, and the novice will probably be all thumbs at first, but perseverance will result in the task being achieved successfully.

As budding is carried out at the peak growing season, during early and midsummer, it is necessary to act quickly to prevent the plant material from drying out. Commercial nurseries usually have their own team of budders, but in addition they will often employ skilled propagators on a piecework basis who are capable of budding several thousands of roses in one day.

Rose stocks are planted in the winter preceding budding. They are one-year-old seedlings usually of a species selected for good rooting qualities and vigor such as *Rosa laxa*, which is the most commonly used rootstock today. A tractor-drawn, manually operated planting machine is used to speed up the process of planting many thousands of the stocks in rows. Once they are planted, the soil on either side will be banked up around them to keep the area needed for budding moist and soft. They will then be left to settle and develop ready for budding to commence in the summer.

When the stocks and the propagation material from existing rose plants are ready, budding will commence. First, the material needed will be cut from the previous crop. Lengths of stem, about 12 in. (30 cm) long and roughly pencil thickness which are mature but not old are cut from the plant. They then have their leaves removed leaving only a piece of the leaf stalk and, for ease of handling. the thorns too are taken off. The stem is then ready for the budder and will be placed, along with other stems of the same variety, in a bucket of water, until it is called for.

In the field a tractor-operated brush will be used to expose the base of the stocks in readiness for the budder. Using a knife specifically designed for the purpose, he or she will make a T-shaped cut in the bark of the stock he is working on, carefully opening it with the back of the part of the blade or handle of the knife designed for this, taking care not to damage the flesh inside. He then skill-fully removes the scion from the stick of bud wood by cutting it away complete with bark and leaf stalk, and then removes the flesh from behind the bark to expose the bud. If there is no bud there, it is discarded. The bud is then inserted into the cut on the stock so that the small piece of leaf stalk is facing upward. Once in place, any surplus bark

1.The scion is carefully sliced away from a stick of bud wood.

2. The propagator trims the scion to the correct length.

3. The pith is removed from under the bark.

4. The tiny budding eye can be seen nestled in the cavity.

5

6

7

8

field before it is dug in the autumn. The likelihood is that it will also supply the grower with bud wood for the next crop.

Budding a rose at home is identical in all respects to commercial budding, except that it is done on a smaller scale. Most growers will be happy to supply you with a few rose stocks but you will have to find your own bud wood, perhaps from a plant you already have, or from a friend or neighbor who has a rose you admire, but cannot purchase. Try to use a proper budding

knife, but if you cannot get the latex ties used by the professionals, secure the bud with raffia instead, wrapping it around the top and the bottom of the T cut.

If you want to propagate a particular rose that has become unobtainable but do not have any faith in your skills at budding, have a word with a rose grower. Most will be happy to bud a few plants for you at a charge similar to other roses of the same type.

5. The stock prepared for budding.

6. A horizontal cut is made in the bark of the stock.

7. A vertical cut is them made to form a T shape.

8. The scion is neatly slid into the bark via the cut.

9. Once in position, the top of the scion is trimmed away so that it is fully in place.

10. A latex patch is secured over the newly inserted bud which will protect the site as the scion fuses with the stock.

11. As the bud begins to grow, the patch will perish and fall away.

above the bud is cut away with the knife at the top of the T cut and it is then bandaged using a latex tie. Another person will usually do the bandaging so that the budder can move on to the next plant.

It soon becomes apparent if the bud has taken or not. If it has fused with the tissue of the rootstock it will begin to shoot, so the nurseryman will carry out a random check by removing some of the latex ties. If there is a large quantity of failures in a particular variety for some reason he may well rebud the stocks using the side of the stock not already budded.

In the autumn, the bud will have developed into a shoot which is trimmed to encourage a bushy plant. Later, the complete top of the stock will be cut away, just above the site of budding, a process growers call "heading back." There is now no possibility of competition for nutrient between the newly added shoot and the branches of the rootstock. By the following summer there is a rose plant, described as a "maiden," which will be grown in the

9

10

11

Grafting

This is another method used by commercial growers, usually to produce the few varieties that are not effectively budded. Once again it is the combining of a host root system with a scion, which together will eventually form one plant.

It is an operation that requires skill, learned through much practice, and the success rate will, by and large, be dependent on this skill. As with budding, the host plant will be chosen so that it influences the growth of the chosen variety, thus creating a successful plant. As with the stocks used for budding, the most common is *Rosa laxa*, usually produced from seed.

In mid-winter, the nurseryman will place around fifty rootstocks in a bundle in damp but sterile peat, under glass to stimulate early root activity. They will remain there for two or three weeks before grafting commences. At this time the bundle will be split and the stocks worked on individually. The top of the stock is removed about 2 in. (5 cm) above the root and a downward cut made into the exposed tissue on one side. The scion will be of one-year-old growth, about 4 in. (10 cm) long and will have been cut on a slant at the top and

bottom. The bottom will then receive an inverted cut so that it matches the cut on the rootstock and they are then slid together, so that the smaller piece of rootstock is held inside the scion. The intention is to introduce the two exposed areas of cambium together, so that they may fuse and become as one. Once this is done, the joint is held together with raffia or grafting tape and then sealed with grafting wax to ensure that the wounds are kept watertight. The top of the scion is also sealed in this way to reduce transpiration.

The newly grafted plant is then splinted with a cane and potted, where it will remain, to begin with in a heated green house, for the duration of the next year. During this time the tape or raffia will be removed to allow the plant to grow without strangulation. Once it is a year old it can be potted or planted outside, depending on whether it is to be sold the following summer or lifted the following autumn as a bare root plant. This method is the most commonly used grafting technique; there are others in which the types of cuts made differ from this, but in all cases the theory of fusing the scion and stock at exposed areas of cambium is the same.

Propagating Roses from Cuttings

Commercial rose growers rarely produce their stock from cuttings. Not only does this method of propagation require masses of material when compared to budding (a cutting is the equivalent to five or more buds), but the rose produced in this way will be slower growing and in many cases will not possess the strength of its budded counterpart. Having said this there are many cases where growing a rose on its own roots is appropriate and, as not every gardener has access to the items needed to bud a rose, it may be the only way of reproducing a plant in the garden.

Hardwood cuttings are the best choice for roses. You should wait until autumn, when the wood has had time enough to ripen during the summer. To liken a cutting to a pencil may seem strange but in all possible cases the wood should be straight, and about the length and thickness of a pencil, do not make it any shorter if you have a choice. The top should be cut at an angle, just above and away from a bud and the bottom cut cleanly below a bud. There are two schools of thought when it comes to the bud at the base. Some suggest that it should be

Cuttings can be placed in pots in the greenhouse or directly into garden soil outside.

cleanly sliced away to expose more cambium (the layer from which the roots will be made) others see this as unnecessary. I have had success with both methods, tending to prefer the second, as a new shoot will form from the base bud. Whichever is chosen, the use of hormone rooting powder will speed up the production of roots.

Find an area of the garden that is sheltered but not waterlogged, and dig a trench deep enough to accommodate about half the length of the cutting. Place a little sharp sand in the base of the trench to stimulate rooting and place the cuttings in it at regular intervals. Infill with the soil removed, firm and water. If you do not have a suitable spot in the garden, the cuttings can be placed in a pot containing equal mixed quantities of soil and sand that has been kept cool in a greenhouse or shed. By early spring in the following year, the cuttings will be making roots and will begin to grow to become small plants. They should be left *in situ* until they become dormant the following autumn when they can be transplanted to their permanent location.

Cuttings can also be made of softer wood during the summer months, but these will require more care. They should be shorter than hardwood cuttings, around 4 in. (10 cm) is ideal, but should be

cut in the same way below a bud at the base and above a bud at the top. Remove all foliage except the two uppermost leaflets, which should be reduced to two leaves to reduce transpiration. Dip the bottom of the cuttings in hormone rooting powder and place them in a pot filled with a mixture of half soil and sand, or a soil substitute such as perlite. Use a hand trowel for this to avoid damaging the delicate wood. Water well and cover with a plastic bag, which should be secured around the top of the pot with a rubber band. This creates the ideal environment for the encouragement of rooting. Place the pot on a tray of well watered pebbles and ensure that this never dries out, the water will travel into the compost of the pot thus preventing dryness occurring here. By autumn, a good if small root system will have developed and the cutting can be moved into a pot containing more nourishing compost in which it can be hardened off during the following spring and summer. By the following autumn it will be large enough to assume its permanent position in the garden.

Above:
1. The branch is pegged into position in a shallow trench.

2. The peg is gently firmed with the foot.

Layering

Layering can be an extremely effective and simple way in which to produce new plants in the garden, but is a propagation method suitable only for roses with long arching growth that can be stretched out to touch the ground, which is why it is an uncommon practice.

Choose wood that is roughly a year old and pull it away from the plant so that it touches the ground at around 12 in. (30 cm) from the growing tip and mark this place on the soil. Allow the branch to spring back up and create a shallow trench at the place marked. Pull the branch

back down and peg it into position in the trench with strong wire. You can, if you wish, wound the bark with a knife to stimulate rooting. Once you have filled in the trench, it is simply a case of waiting for roots to form.

Layering is best done in spring, when growth activity is at its peak and you will have a good idea if rooting has taken place when the protruding tip begins to grow. Check by carefully brushing away some of the soil at the place of pegging. Once roots are established, the parent plant can be detached and the new rose transplanted to a more suitable position, or potted in the following dormant season.

Division

The method of dividing plants for propagation purposes is commonplace with perennial plants and is virtually unheard of with roses. This is because the vast majority of roses are grown on host roots, so any shoots from the ground will be suckers of the rootstock, not of the variety that is apparent above ground level. However, roses that have been grown from seed and varieties growing on their own roots are candidates for this method of increasing roses.

It is not uncommon to find suckers of the old scotch briar roses, albas, *R. rugosas,* and some of the other old roses growing in unexpected situations in old gardens. They are probably nowhere near the site of the original plant which had long since lost all vigor and disappeared. Provided they can be lifted with some root intact they can be moved to other areas of the garden during the dormant season or be potted as gifts for other gardeners.

Micropropagation

It is worth including a few words on this method of propagation as it is likely that more and more roses will be produced this way. It is unlikely, however, that the gardener or nurseryman will ever take part in the practice of it, as micropropagation is a form of tissue culture and, as such, requires sterile laboratory conditions. It is the production of plants from cells extracted from the growing tips of the humble garden rose. These are stimulated to produce more and more growing points until a small plant is formed. Roots are encouraged with the use of hormone agents. Once large enough to handle, the rose is gradually taken off the man-made fibers it is thriving on and encouraged to grow in horticultural composts.

It may well be some time before the practice of micropropagation is common because there are many types of roses that grow less well on their own roots than they do if they are budded or grafted, but there is undoubtedly a place for it. Who knows, one day all plants may be produced in this way and future generations of rose growers may have to have scientific training of some kind.

Above: Young seedling roses ready for growing on.

Growing Roses from Seed

Most garden roses will not come true to their type if propagated from seed but many of the species roses will. Of course, if they have been fertilized by bees or insects carrying pollen the result will be a hybrid and although probably not dissimilar to the parent may display some different characteristics. To prevent this, it is wise to isolate the plant or at least the flower from this possibility. If it is in a pot it should be moved as far away from other roses in the garden as possible, otherwise one or two flowers should be covered with paper cones to prevent outside interference until the blooms have gone over.

Rose breeders will work under glass or in tunnels to speed up the ripening of hips and extend the season in which they have to work but as this sort of control is not possible outside it is likely that only early blooms will provide viable seeds.

Once ripe, the seed pods or hips should be gathered in early autumn and the seeds extracted from them. The hip may contain any number of seeds, from a single specimen to 30 or more. They should then be kept in labeled bags, for six weeks at room temperature and for another six weeks in much cooler temperatures of 34–37°F (1–3°C), often the temperature found in the lower regions of the household refrigerator.

After this period of stratification, they are then ready for sowing. Mix equal quantities of sand with garden compost for this purpose, as the gritty consistency of the sand will help break down the seed coat. You should not plant any deeper than 1 in. (1 cm) below the surface of the compost. If you have the benefit of heated greenhouse benches, they will speed up germination if set to 54–60°F (12–16°C). Germination ceases at around 82°F (28°C).

Seedlings emerge with two rounded leaves which are almost succulent in appearance. It is best to wait until true leaves have appeared before potting them on. Transplant into small pots or plugs to prevent them being overwatered and use, where possible, a soil-based compost, growing them on in pots throughout the following summer. After this, they can be potted on further or given a permanent position in the garden.

Professional growers rarely grow roses from seed, as the time consumed in production of salable plants in this way would be huge and the results are all too variable. The only times this is not so is in the process of breeding new varieties and in the production of rose stocks. Rose stocks are developed in this way because the possibility of viral infection is diminished.

Below: A newly germinated rose seedling.

Breeding roses

All rose nurseries introduce new roses on a regular basis, whether bred by themselves or an independent breeder. They do so for two reasons above all: the first is to fulfil the demand of the gardening public for ever better roses, although each and every one of us has preconceived ideas as to perfection, they can at least concentrate on major areas such as perfume and disease resistance; the second is for publicity purposes, as a new rose named after a famous celebrity or charity to which they are donating profits is far more likely to attract the attention of the public than the others in their catalog and they will be remembered for having introduced that rose. Coupled with this is the fact that new roses are usually shown to the public for the first time at flower shows, where many other rose growers are also exhibiting. As in everything there is much friendly competition between growers all hoping to gain media coverage of a new rose introduction at a show which, in turn, will bring in business.

The hybridizing of roses is a complex subject and it is very easy to get bogged down in the botanical logic of genetics that dictates its success. It is possible to obtain excellent results with only a little knowledge, and this is per-haps the best way to approach the subject. One can spend hours researching chromosomes and family trees when, frankly, it is just as well get on with the practical aspect of the work, as many of the resulting seedlings will be a disappointment regardless of the time spent working out which are compatible parents. As a busy person, this is how I approach the subject. I use the knowledge I have of the idiosyncrasies of individual roses, coupled with my appreciation of their beauty when choosing which two should be put together. After a while, you get to know which make good parents, which set hips well, which encourage early germination, and so on.

Most professional breeders will have a tunnel or greenhouse in which they house plants for the purpose of breeding. It is best to keep them under such cover as the rose hip, from which the seed is extracted, takes some time to ripen before the seed is viable. By housing the plants in warm conditions, you are able to start work earlier in the year and the hips will also be encouraged to ripen more quickly. It is also easier to control pests and diseases in a confined area, although the heat and poor air circulation found in these places often encourage such plagues, so care has to be taken to deter them thoroughly.

The roses will usually be grown in soil-based compost in large pots but sometimes they will be planted directly into the ground. Where there are rose plants planted into the soil there may be problems with overwintering pests and diseases and, of course, they can not be easily replaced with another variety because of replant disease.

The roses to be used for breeding should at all times be kept well watered and fed, with a high potash feed. A rose that is struggling will not produce good quantities of flowers and will, subsequently, struggle to set hips, it will also be more prone to disease which, in turn, may affect the ability of the plant to produce hips. Pests and diseases should be carefully monitored and dealt with and a regular regime of control should be adopted even before there is any apparent sign of them.

One of the most common pests in the greenhouse or tunnel is the red spider mite which will move in, often unnoticed, in midsummer and then thrive in the dry still conditions, constructing delicate webs on hips and leaves. In a severe attack this troublesome pest will cause the loss of some or all hips. Refer to the chapter on pests and diseases for suggestions on its control.

Roses for breeding should be placed in the tunnel or greenhouse in the spring, to encourage early flowering. If the plants to be worked on are in the garden this is clearly not possible but it may be possible to erect a polythene structure over them to force them on, as the earlier the pollination can take place the sooner the hip will be ripe. Good husbandry is important from the beginning to encourage blooms, so feed at this time.

Once flowers begin to emerge, the pollination process can begin. The selected blooms on the female or mother parent (that which will produce the hips) should be between the stages of bud and open flower, when insects will have been unable to penetrate and pollinate the flower, thereby upsetting the planned cross. The petals should be removed, usually by grasping them and tearing them off all at once. If the odd petal remains, this too should be removed, as it is the coloring of the petal that attracts insects in the first place. It is now necessary to emasculate the plant to prevent self pollination. Do this by cutting off the all anthers; a small pair of manicure scissors are ideal for this. Be diligent in this task, for just a few remaining anthers could spoil your work. The prepared flowers should be left in this state until the following day when the stigma will have become sticky in preparation for the arrival

Opposite:
1. The petals of the female flower are stripped away.

2. The stamens are removed using a pair of manicure scissors or a knife.

of the pollen. This sticky secretion will cause the pollen to adhere to the stigma and will assist in the forming of a pollen tube, which will pass through the stigma and enter the ovaries which are hidden in the receptacle.

After twenty-four hours the female parent should be pollinated. The pollen needed is often seen as a fine dust on the inner petals of roses but if you are unsure as to whether the pollen on your chosen male parent is ready, gently touch the anthers with your fingers. Ripe pollen will come away on them. There are two ways in which the pollen can be transferred to the female parent. One is to collect the pollen, placing it in a container in which, if airtight, the pollen will last for 24 hours or longer given low temperatures, and applying it with a brush so that the stigma is visibly covered. Breeders who pollinate on a large scale will often collect the unripe anthers as they emasculate and keep them in a container until the pollen bursts from them, usually within 48 hours. The second way of transferring the pollen is to select a flower with ripe pollen, fold the petals back so that the anthers are foremost and brush these against the stigma of the mother parent. The latter is an efficient method only if there are large enough numbers of desirable roses available to guarantee pollen availability and, as I am lucky enough to

have large numbers of roses at my disposal, this is the method I favor. It reduces the task to two stages with no need to worry about the care of stored pollen and eliminates the necessity of keeping a number of cleaned brushes on hand.

Once the pollen has been applied to the extent that you can see a dusty covering on the stigma, a label should be attached. I find it best to indicate both parents on the label with the female name first. If you follow the discipline of always placing the variety first on the label you will begin to gather much valuable information for future reference. You will be able to determine the qualities of one parent against another as your experience increases and you gather personal knowledge and research in your own work, assuming you are serious; there are many commercially available but amateur-bred roses.

Once labeled, it is a waiting game. Some hips may not develop but there are often different reasons for this. It may be that the two roses were not compatible for reasons such as their individual chromosome counts. Disease, lack of water, poor nutrition, too little pollen, bad weather, and pests are all possible causes, any one of which may cause an isolated plant to suffer. Therefore do not expect perfect results, it is all part of the challenge.

By early autumn, after around sixteen weeks, the hips will be seen to be ripe and are ready for harvesting. There may be some hips that have not yet developed their autumn coloring, but if they are plump and fleshy it is still worth harvesting them. Collect the hips with labels firmly attached and take them indoors, or to a comfortable location, where the seed may be extracted; if there are many this is a time consuming task. Carefully cut through the outer flesh of the hip so that you may pull it apart in two halves. The seed will then be visible. Numbering from one to thirty or more, they are the hard, usually rounded kernels found within the fleshy pith. Use a knife to evacuate them into a container and wash them under the tap with the aid of a sieve. They should now be transferred into sealable polythene bags or other suitable sealable containers containing damp sand or a damp soil substitute such as vermiculite. The aggressive nature of these will help break down the seed coat (a layer on the outer shell which breaks down according to various natural factors such as frost, thus allowing germination of seeds separately over a long term to, in nature's way, protect the species) through which the seedling plant will break out.

The seeds should be stored for around six weeks at room temperature and then for a following six weeks at a temperature of 34–37°F (1–3° C), often found in the lower area of the household fridge. After this period of storage they are ready for sowing. I sow seeds in trays with individual cells, which allow the roots to establish to some extent before transplanting, but seed trays are also recommended, provided that transplantation takes place before rooting invades the space of another seed, thus upsetting its chances.

The initial leaves of the rose seedling, the first to be seen, are in a pair, fleshy and almost succulent in appearance. They will remain for a day or two before more characteristic leaves begin to appear. Once there are one or two sets of true leaves present, the plant can be moved into a small pot. Do not use any container bigger than needed in order to save time later on, as you will be tempted to water to the compost's capacity, which will be too much for the rose seedling. As the seedling grows, it will begin to display its future characteristics in leaf form and color. If you have been lucky enough to develop a rose with repeat or continuous-flowering capabilities, it is likely to produce a bloom in its first year of life; although this will be smaller than the true bloom it usually correctly shows color, form, and sometimes scent.

The new rose will need to be grown on in its pot and hardened off outdoors until it is large enough to provide propagation material. The best way to increase its numbers is by budding, as

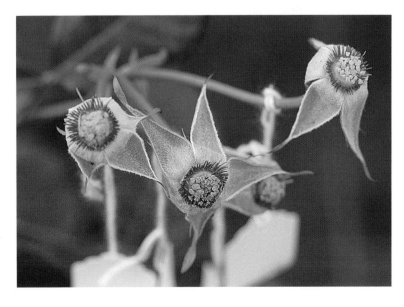

it will then assume the characteristics it will portray should it be good enough for commercial production but if these facilities are unavailable, a few successfully rooted cuttings will cover the possibility of the loss of the original seedling plant. The resulting roses should then be grown on under trial to ascertain whether or not the seedling possesses enough good qualities for introduction to the market place.

Commercially, new seedlings are included in the general propagation carried out by nurserymen and then planted in a trial bed where they will remain for several years prior to possible introduction so that the description of the rose in the grower's catalogue is accurate. Once it is decided that the rose is suitable for introduction, it will be budded in large numbers, over a two or three year period to build up enough stock of it and it will be registered with the necessary bodies, in particular the American Rose Society, under a trade name. A suitable name will be chosen for the rose

a year or two preceding its introduction, either one that has been chosen by the grower or a name which has been requested by a charity body or private individual.

On a smaller scale, the amateur will need to approach a grower to introduce a new rose for them. The grower will still have to propagate it in order to build up enough stock and will want to put it on trial it for a period to ensure that it has standards applicable to the status of the grower. He may also want to be responsible for the naming of it but this would be done in consultation with the breeder. Roses bred by an individual but introduced by a grower should also be registered under a trade name.

If you wish to breed new roses for your own pleasure only, this is a delightful and rewarding pastime. The plants can be given a name chosen by yourself and make delightful, unique gifts for family and friends.

Pests, Diseases, and

other Rose Ailments

Problems associated with roses are often the first reason gardeners give for not growing them, but this should not be the case. Rarely is a rose so susceptible to a disease or heavy infestation of pests that it is spoiled, and if it does get a little black spot or mildew is it really that important? Nearly all plants are prone to one thing or another, and we must not allow such problems to spoil our appreciation of them. Having said this, there are occasions when pests and diseases can get out of control, and in these instances it is hard to ignore them nor indeed should you, for the results can be devastating.

Prevention is always better than cure; the use of chemicals in the garden is a controversial issue and, where there is a choice, I prefer to be as organic as possible. There are some chemicals available for use in the treatment of roses that are kinder than others, not killing friendly insects, for example, and these are as good as their more cruel counterparts. Remember, however, that roses can develop a resistance to a particular substance so it is wise to alternate types used.

If you do choose to spray your roses in order to control their susceptibility, a regular regime is important. There is absolutely no point in an occasional blitz, especially when dealing with disease, as most fungicides are systemic (working from within the plant) and will loose their strength after a couple of weeks. Many insecticides, however, work on contact so if insects are the only problem you can treat only when they are present. There are chemicals available that will deal with pests and diseases at the same time, working just as well as two independent sprays. If you cannot bear the thought of using chemicals in the garden you must select healthy varieties to begin with and look after them well. A well fed and tended rose is much less likely to fall prey to disease than a neglected one.

As well as chemical insecticides, there are organic pest-control sprays available. They work by coating the pest in a fatty acid and are obviously a lot more environmentally friendly.

Diseases

Black spot

Black spot must be the best known disease of roses and there are varieties, as well as areas of the country, that are more prone than others. City center dwellers may have less of a problem than those living in the countryside, as pollution tends to keep it at bay. The black spot spore is airborne and will settle on leaves where it causes a black or dark colored mark to form. These soon spread across the whole leaf, eventually causing it to fall onto younger stems, which become mottled and may wither. The disease may also be spread by using infected garden implements, such as pruning shears.

The only effective control is to use a fungicide on a regular basis, at least once every other week, from early in the season when the roses have begun to produce leaves and certainly before signs of the disease are apparent. Always follow the instructions carefully when using chemicals, both for safety and effective use. There are other measures that will help prevent reinfection. Always clear away any diseased leaves that have fallen to the ground as they will be covered in the tiny spores that have the potential to overwinter so as to be ready to infect the following season. A badly

Black spot first appears as small dark blemishes on the leaf which quickly multiply.

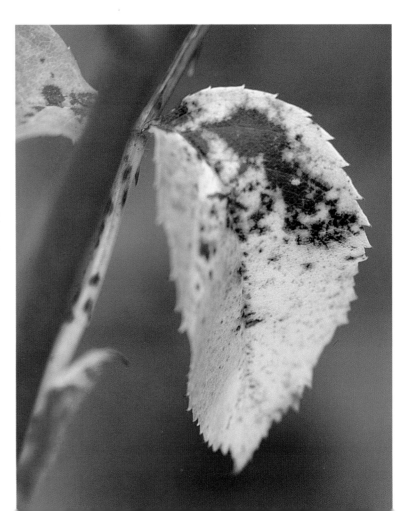

affected plant can be washed with mild sterilent during the dormant season, and it is wise to also wash down any supports the rose may be against, as the disease can harbor there also.

Mildew

There are two forms of mildew found on roses. The most common is powdery mildew, and can be found on roses from fairly early in the season. It shows itself as powdery gray to white patches on young shoots and leaves, causes them to curl and prevents their growth. If it is not dealt with quickly, the whole plant can become effected.

A plant suffering from mildew not only has distorted growth but is far more prone to other diseases, such as rust and black spot. There are contact and systemic sprays available, and if a plant is known to be a sufferer they should be used well before there are any signs of it.

Mildew likes dry, still locations and will spread extremely rapidly in such situations, therefore try only to plant resistant varieties against walls or in very sheltered places. A regular wash down, morning and evening, from the hose and keeping the plant well watered may help keep mildew at bay, but if you intend to be totally organic, take advice on the most healthy varieties before planting roses in the garden.

Downy mildew can be a problem on roses growing in greenhouses, caused by the extremes of day and night time temperatures coupled with poor ventilation. It is unlikely to appear on roses growing in the garden. Patches of brown or bluish gray appear on mature leaves causing them to fall and on occasion will spread to the stems. The only effective control is to use fungicide but if the problem is not great, the infected leaves should simply be removed and destroyed.

Rust

Rust, probably the most harmful of all rose diseases, can often creep into the garden unnoticed as the small bright orange pustules attach themselves to the less visible undersides of leaves. Here they will multiply rapidly, spreading all over the plant and sometimes even onto the stems. As they mature they change color through brown to black and will kill the leaf that supports them, causing it to fall to the ground. If the infection is bad, the results can be heartbreaking: the rose will loose all its leaves and could die.

Action must be taken at the first noticed sign of its arrival. Firstly remove all infected leaves and destroy them. Then spray, either with a general purpose rose fungicide or a chemical that is more specific; a

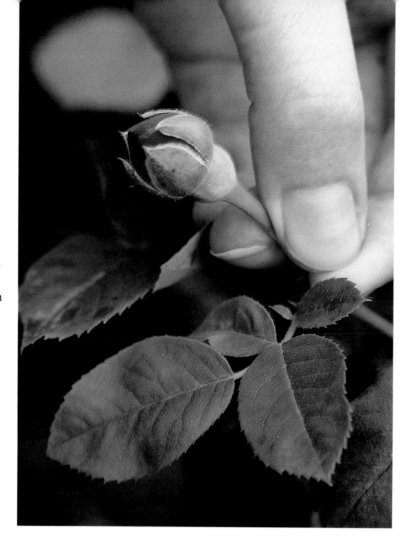

Mildew often appears around flower buds.

look along the shelves of your local plant retailer will show you which to go for. Ensure that no fallen infected leaves are left, and gather and destroy them also. A winter wash with a sterilizing chemical to cover the rose, the surrounding soil, and any supports the rose is dependant on may help rid overwintering spores. If you have plants that suffer badly from rust year after year, it would be best to remove them from the garden as they will cause the disease to spread to varieties that are usually not effected.

Stem canker

Stem canker is most often found on older plants, especially those that have developed much older wood. It is also seen on younger plants that have had the benefit of regular pruning over the years, where such wounds have allowed the entry of the disease. It may seem strange that I advocate regular pruning but now report a drawback to doing so, but canker is easily dealt with and an uncommon enough phenomena that it should not deter the gardener from pruning. Stem canker manifests itself in the form of large gnarled lesions, usually irregular in shape with shallow edges, swelling toward the center and often with lifting areas of bark. The only available treatment is their removal. If in awkward, structurally important places the lesion should be cleanly removed with a knife to expose uninfected tissue and the wound then dressed with grafting wax so that it may heal, although in an older plant this may not work. If the canker appears on an area of stem that can be easily removed without detriment to the plant then this is the obvious solution. Total avoidance of stem canker is impossible, but keeping wounds clean by using sharp implements when pruning will help.

Pests

Aphids

Aphids must rank as the biggest pest nuisance in the world of roses. They come in a variety of colors, but the most persistent are the greenflies that love to gather and feed in large numbers on young shoots and flower buds. It is the sticky secretion, named honeydew, left behind that is perhaps the most annoying aspect of them as is not

Above: Aphids collect on soft young growth and flower buds.

Right: Caterpillars eat away portions of leaves.

only unsightly but coats the affected areas of the plant, covering breathing pores, and therefore restricting natural growth. In bad cases, the honey-dew may develop sooty mold which is black in color and most unsightly. In days gone by, gardeners would purchase special brushes to remove the aphids or would spray them with soapy water, a method of control which is still considered worth trying today. Until recently the only sure way of ridding the garden of these pests was the use of insecticide, but there are now organic sprays available containing fatty acids which seem to do a good job. The most efficient natural predator is the ladybug and many garden birds enjoy picking them off as well, but they will never get rid of them completely, especially in a bad attack.

Capsid bugs
Less common than aphids, these annoying insects enjoy dining on the young growing shoots and leaves of roses. The effect is that the growth becomes stunted and is left full of tiny holes. The only method of control is to use a systemic insecticide, but as they move around swiftly from one plant to another they may be difficult to eradicate.

Caterpillars
Caterpillars do not seem to have a very fussy diet, seeming to enjoy any greenery in the garden and this includes the leaves of roses. Whole sections of leaf may be seen to have

Above: Cuckoo spit is a protective substance housing the nymph of the froghopper.

disappeared, almost overnight. There are chemicals available to control infestations but as caterpillars are the larvae of moths, the task is a hard one. A search of the plant for the offender followed by its disposal may be the best solution.

Cuckoo spit
It is not unusual to find a spittle-like foamy substance nestled in the leaf joints of roses. It is perhaps not a delight to the eye but is insignificant in itself as it is actually the home of the froghopper nymph, which is relatively harmless. If it is considered too unsightly, the best method of removal is to give it a sudden blast from the garden hose. Otherwise given time, it will disappear.

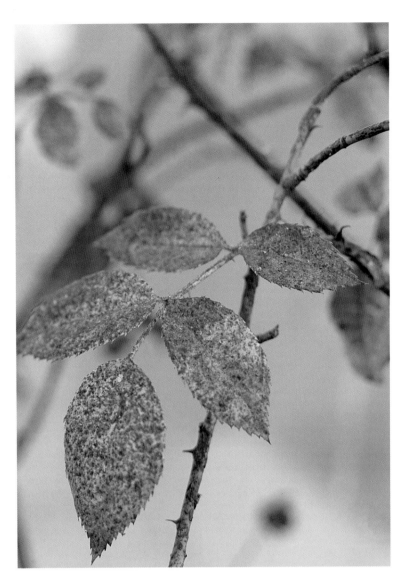

Red spider mite

This little pest can cause many problems in greenhouses and occasionally, during the hottest of summers, on plants in the garden that are in very sheltered situations. Red spider mites love to be active in very dry and airless conditions, which is why they are most prolific in mid-summer onward. Invisible to all but the most scrutinizing eye, they will often have been present for a while before evidence is found in the form of very fine webs between leaflets and around buds. They live on the undersides of the leaves, which is another reason for their apparent invisible arrival. They will cause the egg laden leaves to become dusty and limp before falling to the ground where they will overwinter and hatch the following year. Eggs will also lay dormant in the fabric of greenhouses and tunnels to re-emerge there the following year. Control is difficult and there is only one chemical with

**Above:
Red spider mites love hot airless conditions and are most troublesome in greenhouses.**

**Right:
Leaf-rolling sawflies lay their eggs on the surface of leaves, which then become curled as protection for the eggs.**

supremacy of control, Pirimiphos-methyl, but the newly emerging organic sprays now also claim to rid roses of spider mite. I pen this at a time of year when I have no possibility of experimenting with said sprays against the culprit and will therefore give no evidence as to the success of them, suffice to say that they are worth trying.

Sawfly

There are at least three different types of sawfly that enjoy roses, but two by far more damaging.

Leaf-rolling sawfly has the potential to completely distort all the leaves on and thus render unsightly any individual plant. The adult female will lay her eggs on the leaf, while at the same time injecting them with a chemical to cause them to completely curl for the protection of her offspring. Control is often impossible, for the damage will have been created before visible signs emerge. Spraying regimes with systemic fungicide in the early summer may help, but the only other solution is to wait for leaves to fall or remove them until they are replaced by fresh growth. There is no great harm caused to the plant although it may be weakened somewhat and perhaps a little more prone to disease.

The slug sawfly behaves differently and is perhaps a little easier to control. It enjoys dining on rose leaves, relishing the fleshy parts but leaving the veins to form a skeleton leaf, a weird and bewildering sight when it has devoured many leaves on one plant. Although less common than the leaf-rolling sawfly, its treatment is the same and usually more successful.

Thrips

Thrips love the tight full buds of some types of roses and will disfigure them by nibbling around the edges of petals. The damage they cause is cosmetic and by no means a detriment to growth and as they tend to appear only spasmodically, usually during thundery weather, it is as well to just put up with them. If, however, they are proving such a nuisance that you cannot overlook them you will need to spray the early opening buds with insecticide.

Animal pests

If you live in the countryside it is likely that your roses may, at some time or another, suffer damage caused by rabbits, deer, and farm animal grazing in fields adjacent to gardens. I have also heard of, but not personally experienced, squirrels damaging roses.

Rabbits love to nibble at young succulent growth and can be a major nuisance, preventing young plants from assuming proper growth and causing older ones to be bare at the base. Control of rabbits is almost impossible because they breed so quickly and if they cannot be kept out of the garden you will need to put protection of some form around your roses, at least near the base.

Deer and grazing animals also enjoy the flavor of roses and if you have

them growing as a boundary, either as a hedge or in the form of climbers and ramblers on fences they are likely to be at risk. Deer are likely to strike in mid-winter when most hungry and are a bigger problem in the United States than in Britain. The only precaution one can take is to plant the thorniest of varieties, but these can still be at risk if the animals are hungry enough.

Moles can also be a pest to roses, especially if they are present in large numbers, by tunneling under roots and damaging them. There are several ways of ridding the garden of moles and it may be worth trying one of the old fashioned methods, the most popular of which is to place and empty bottle in the tunnel beneath a mole hill. The sound of the wind as it blows across the top of the bottle is said to cause the moles to move on.

Proliferation is a malformation of the flowers usually seen early in the flowering season.

Other rose ailments

Viruses

Viruses are transmitted at the time of propagation and have nothing to do with the husbandry of the rose in the garden. It is more likely that the rootstock used during propagation in years gone by infected a variety and this variety has gone on to be the strain available now. Today the majority of growers will use rootstock grown from seed, which, by and large, prevents viruses being spread to offspring but, if the budded cultivar had already been infected, there is no prevention and the newly resulting rose plant will share the same traits. Exactly what these are, no one can be sure. The most prevalent symptoms of virus are irregularities in the leaf, for example wavy yellow lines across the surface, but flower quality can be affected too. Malcolm Manners, of the Citrus Institute, Florida Southern College, who has worked long and hard on this subject, has produced virus-free forms of the older roses we both love and respect, with stunningly larger flowers than would be expected, perhaps true to their original form. One day perhaps he or another scientist will give us the answers and all reproduced roses will be the same as their original predecessors.

It is often the case that a rose will appear perfectly healthy for a large part of its life but with no warning, will suddenly show signs of having a virus. It is this occurrence that led to the belief that viruses were some sort of contagious problem, but we can be sure that viruses are not spread in the way fungal diseases are. As this is the case, there is no reason to worry about a rose with the problem, it is simply a case of having to live with it.

Proliferation

Proliferated flowers can cause much alarm when seen for the first time. Some of the very double, old-fashioned roses will develop an extra bud, or on occasion buds, from the center of the flower.

These buds will be seen to be perfect examples and will often be attached to a short stem from the center of the flower. There is dispute as to the cause of this malformation, some say that it is a virus and others that it is some genetic mutation; what is more certain is that there are factors that affect the severity of it. Plants grown in shady situations seem to suffer more than their counterparts in more open places or those grown under glass. It also seems to occur more often after a cold spring. Repeat-flowering varieties seldom show signs of it in their second flush, so the only treatment for these is to remove the offensive blooms that appear earlier in the year and wait for later ones to arrive. If it occurs on once-flowering varieties, the situation is more grave as there will be no second blooming to look forward to.

Spray damage

Although largely common sense, it is useful to include a word about spray damage. Roses are very susceptible to even the tiniest amounts of weed killer and if this is used in the garden it should be applied when there is little or no breeze to prevent it drifting onto garden roses. Always use a separate sprayer for this purpose for no matter how well it is washed out, there are always minor traces of it left, enough to cause damage. Of course, if spraying is being carried out in adjacent fields you will have no control over drifting and the resulting damage will manifest itself in the form of distorted growth, and in very bad cases even death of the plant.

Scorch

Scorch on rose leaves is more unsightly than any great detriment to the plant. It is likely to be more apparent on roses growing under cover that have been placed too close to the glass or polythene or that have had their leaves watered during sun. Outside it can occur when there has been full sun after rain, but this is less likely. Leaves will become brown and papery around their edges and if badly affected will fall. If watering roses with a hose or can, try to do so in the morning or evening when the sun's rays are less powerful.

Balled flowers

Balling of flowers usually occurs when there has been rain followed by sun, or when the atmosphere is generally damp. Outer petals on full-flowered roses become fused together when wet and the effect of the sun is to cook the damp petals so that they form a shell around the flower. If action is not taken all the petals will eventually turn brown and the flower will fall to the ground.

If you have time and have perhaps only a few affected roses, the outer petals can be gently teased open to allow the remainder of the flower to form naturally.

Chlorosis

Yellowing and the appearance of pale patches on the leaf are often caused by mineral deficiencies; usually iron and magnesium are the elements most responsible. To ensure the well being of the rose, an attempt should be made to correct the situation. If the plant is suffering from iron deficiency, often indicated by yellowing leaves, an application of sequested iron or a feeding of liquid seaweed with added iron will normally redress the situation. Epson salts are available from most drugstores and will cure magnesium deficiency, which causes leaves to develop pale patches between the veins.

**Above:
The tinest droplet of weedkiller can cause rose leaves to become highly disfigured. Always avoid spraying if there is a breeze**

**Right:
Leaves can easily become scorched if there is very hot sun after rain. Dark red and deep pink flowers can fade in strong sunlight. This rose, 'Souvenir du Docteur Jamain,' is best planted in the shade**

Plant Directory

Classification of Rose Types

The genus *Rosa* is a hugely complicated one, but a total understanding of its complexity is not needed to appreciate the merits of individual roses. A breakdown of the various groups can help to compare the value of one group with another, so for the purposes of this directory I have classified them into "family" groups, where those included in each group are in some way related and similar in habit and form. One group may be closely related to another and, although this may be occasionally apparent, is not especially relevant when it comes to selecting roses for the garden.

This directory is divided, firstly according to the nature of the roses included, into bush, shrub climbing and rambling roses and then, within each of these headings, into the family groups there contained. Many of the older groups have a name that refers in some way to one of the original species roses from which the group developed. In more recent times, however, the name given refers more to the style of the roses in that group or in the case of a diverse group they are referred to using a broader group name, such as the modern shrub roses. It is not possible to describe every rose in current existence, for such a task would be near impossible. Included in each group, however, are the most important of each, both in garden worthiness and their role in the importance of the group. Although not every member of that group is described, I have included where possible a cross section of varieties to show the choice available.

Flowering Seasons

In all descriptions, reference is made to the flowering season. As a guide, summer-flowering roses produce one abundant flush of blooms, repeat-flowering varieties will provide more than one flush and continuous-flowering varieties will flower intermittently throughout the season. The date of introduction is given where known and in all cases the size given is height before spread. Sizes are for an average mature plant; it may be that soil and climate differences cause the rose to vary from the sizes stated.

Bush or Bedding Roses

These generally fall into two categories: hybrid teas and floribundas, although there are many roses described in the shrub section that can be used in the same way as these. They are not so fashionable now, but these are the roses used in large beds of singular or mixed varieties and in other more formal planting. They are also useful in tubs or in mixed planting in borders. Hybrid teas and floribundas are often referred to as modern roses but the definition of modern roses is controversial. Some consider that the date of the introduction of the first hybrid tea 'La France' should be the point from which the modern rose dates, but this was in 1865 and I personally do not think that everything from 1865 can be described as modern. My preference is to use the Second World War as a cut-off date, the convention used by several eminent rosarians.

Hybrid teas or large-flowered roses

Two titles are applied to this group of roses. Early hybrid teas were, indeed, hybrids of the tea roses, but, over the years their genealogy has become more complicated leading to a new name of large-flowered roses, but I, like many, find it difficult to think of them as anything but hybrid teas.

They are a huge group of roses and remain extremely popular with gardeners. They are ideal for cutting as they usually bear solitary blooms, but a few are available that produce small clusters. Among them can be found colors for every taste, and many exude a perfume. They are a useful group of roses that are usually quite bushy and free flowering. There are also some climbing hybrid teas described later in this directory.

'Anna Pavlova'

This variety has a most delicious perfume that is almost overpowering. Full blooms are soft blush pink from pointed buds and leaves are leathery, dark green, and rounded in shape. It is tall for a hybrid tea and can be quite slender. Try to avoid planting it in poor soil or shade.
Beales, UK, 1981, continuous flowering, 4 x 3 ft. (1.2 x 1 m)

'Fragrant Cloud'

The double orangy-red flowers of this hybrid tea are deeply scented. Foliage is dark and glossy, with plum-colored young shoots. An upright growing variety.
Tantau, Germany 1964 Continuous flowering 30 x 24 ft. (75 x 60 cm)

'Just Joey'

The flowers on this rose are large, blowsy, and petals are wavy edged. Its coppery-orange coloring makes it stand out in the garden, where it is very free flowering. Leaves are dark and glossy, if a little sparse, and growth is strong. This is an excellent rose.
Cant, UK, 1972, continuous flowering, 24 x 24 in. (60 x 60 cm)

Although 'Frangrant Cloud' was introduced in 1964, it is still very popular today.

'La France'

I include this as it was the first of its type to be introduced, although it is no more outstanding than many other hybrid teas. Full flowers are mid-silvery pink and are very highly perfumed. It displays upright growth, which carries mid-green leaves.
Guillot Fils, France, 1865, repeat flowering, 4 x 3 ft. (1.2 x 1 m)

'Mrs. Oakley Fisher'

Several single varieties were introduced in the early part of the 20th century, and this is one of my favorites. The flowers are best described as apricot with a bold ring of bright orange stamens. Young growth and leaves are plum colored, a lovely contrast to the flowers.
Cant, UK, 1921, continuous flowering, 24 x 24 in. (60 x 60 cm)

'Ophelia'

'Ophelia' is one of the most beautiful older hybrid teas. The fully double, pointed blooms are soft creamy pink with a tinge of lemon at the base and are scented. When open, the flower displays a magnificent circle of amber gold stamens. Foliage is large and leathery. Also similar are 'Lady Sylvia' and 'Mme. Butterfly,' both sports of it.
W.Paul, 1912, continuous flowering 24 x 24 in. (60 x 60 cm)

'Royal William'

Deep velvety red, fully double blooms are well scented and remain high centered, even when fully open. A good rose for cutting, on an upright plant with plentiful dark green foliage.
Kordes, Germany, 1984, continuous flowering, 30 x 24 in. (75 x 60 cm)

Floribundas or Cluster-Flowered Roses

As with the hybrid teas, floribundas have also been given a new title but I find "cluster-flowered roses" much more cumbersome than "floribundas" so with this I shall stick. Perhaps these words will roll off the tongues of future generations with ease. These roses, by whatever name you give them, are free flowering and support masses of blooms in clusters. They are ideal for mass planting but have other uses also. They are also successful if planted in tubs or in mixed planting with other shrubs and perennials and the longer stemmed varieties are also good as cut blooms.

'Lili Marlene' has abundant flowers that are velvety in texture.

'Amber Queen'
This is an excellent little rose and, judging by the number of awards it has received, I am not alone in this opinion. Many-petaled blooms are golden-amber amid dark, glossy leaves on a bushy plant. This shorter-growing floribunda is at home anywhere and will be happy in a tub or at the front of the border.
Harkness, UK, 1984, continuous flowering, 24 x 24 in. (60 x 60 cm)

'Korresia'
Bright, clear yellow blooms are well sized and held in large clusters. Leaves are large and healthy, glossy mid-green. 'Korresia' is a stocky, sturdily growing plant.
Kordes, Germany, 1977, continuous flowering, 24 x 24 in. (60 x 60 cm)

'Lili Marlene'
Double flowers are cupped and open, rich velvety red with bright anthers. It is very free flowering, producing its blooms in large clusters. It does not get huge and makes a good specimen in a small tub. Growth is bushy with well armed stems, and leaves are dark leathery green.
Kordes, Germany, 1959, continuous flowering, 24 x 30 in. (60 x 75 cm)

'Margaret Merril'
White flowers are gently flushed pink. Buds are very pointed until the bloom opens, when pronounced golden anthers are revealed. A special feature of this lovely rose is its superb perfume. Foliage is dark and growth upright.
Harkness, UK, 1977, continuous flowering, 30 x 24 in. (75 x 60 cm)

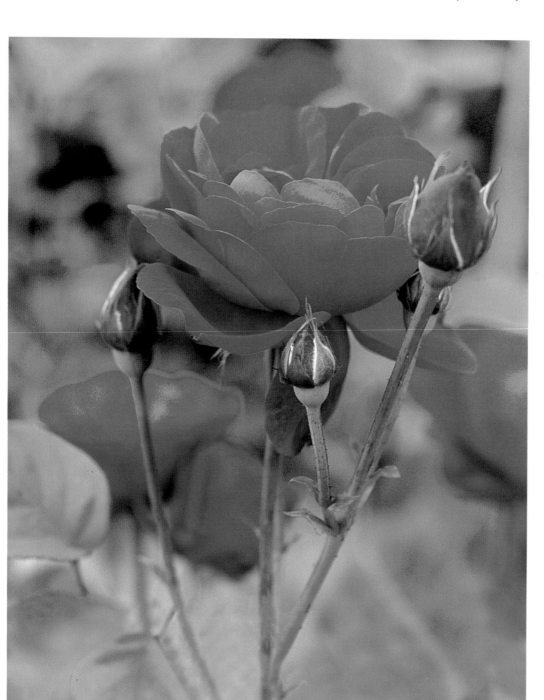

'Norwich Castle'

Flowers are a lovely shade of coppery orange and are double, opening flat and fading to a soft apricot-orange as they mature. Leaves are light to mid-green and growth upright in habit. A very free-flowering variety.
Beales, UK, 1979, continuous flowering, 30 x 24 in. (75 x 60 cm)

'Plentiful'

Although a modern rose, the style of the flowers is old fashioned. They are packed with very deep pink petals, which form a quartered appearance. Leaves are leathery, a little coarse, and dark green in color. A thorny plant.
LeGrice, UK, 1961, continuous flowering, 30 x 30 in. (75 x 75 cm)

'Queen Elizabeth'

'Queen Elizabeth' is one of the most famous of all floribundas. Everything about it is big: the flowers, leaves, and growth are all larger than average. Double flowers emerge from long pointed buds and are soft clear pink with a little perfume, and are arranged in clusters. The large leaves are dark and glossy and the growth is upright and tall for its type. 'Queen

Elizabeth' makes a good hedge or boundary in places where it is not possible to have a wide hedge.
Lammerts, USA, 1954, continuous flowering, 5 x 2¹/₂ ft. (1.5 m x 75 cm)

'Twenty-fifth'

This variety produces masses of deep blood red, semidouble, open flowers in large clusters regularly throughout the summer months. Each open bloom displays a fine coronet of golden yellow stamens. Foliage is dark, glossy, and healthy. A healthy and useful little rose.
Beales, UK, 1996, continuous flowering, 24 x 24 in. (60 x 60 cm)

'Twenty Fifth' is an excellent all-round bedding rose.

Miniature Floribundas
or Patio Roses

The name patio rose was given to a group of roses that are really just compact floribundas, with the intention of making gardeners aware that roses can be grown in a pot on the patio. This group of roses make good specimens in tubs, but they are not the only ones with this capability; all roses, even vigorous ramblers can be grown in a pot with some degree of success, provided they are well fed and watered. It is also the case that patio roses can be grown elsewhere in the garden, at the front of the border or as a specimen plant in a small garden.

'Apricot Sunblaze'

This rose has a dense habit with small glossy leaves. Bright orange-red blooms, which are at first cupped, open flat and display many petals. Mostly borne in clusters although it is possible to find the odd singular flower.
Saville, USA, 1984, continuous flowering, 15 x 10 in. (38 x 25 cm)

'Dresden Doll'

Soft pink flowers are semidouble, cupped and emerge from heavily mossed buds in clusters. Stems are also covered in moss which, if touched, is slightly scented. This is a compact and unusual rose.
Moore, USA, 1975, continuous flowering, 12 x 10 in. (30 x 25cm)

'Regensberg'

Large double flowers are bright cerise-pink with white streaks and edging and at their centers. The reverse of the petals is also silvery white. It is one of the so-called hand-painted roses for which this breeder is well known.
McGredy, New Zealand, 1979, continuous flowering, 18 x 18 in. (45 x 45 cm)

'Robin Redbreast'

Semidouble red flowers have central creamy white centers and appear in bunches in great profusion throughout the summer. Leaves are glossy and mid green on thorny stems. Inclined to spreading growth.
Ilsink, Netherlands, 1984, continuous flowering, 18 x 18 in. (45 x 45 cm)

'Sweet Dream'

Soft peachy-apricot blooms are double and prettily formed in a cupped style. Usually borne in clusters although there may be a few singular blooms. Dense foliage is very glossy and reasonably resistant to disease. Growth compact.
Fryer, UK, 1988, continuous flowering, 18 x 12 in. (45 x 30 cm)

Miniature Roses

Miniatures were popular at the beginning of the 19th century, but there were few colors available at this time and they soon became unfashionable. Cultivation of them ceased until the 1920s when 'Rouletii' was discovered in Switzerland, and so began a new era of popularity in which new miniatures were raised. It is best to purchase miniatures that have been developed on their own roots, as these roses will be smaller than their equivalent counterparts that have been budded or grafted. Although often sold as houseplants, they do not respond well to being grown indoors. They can be successful in window boxes or as edging to beds and borders.

'Cinderella'
A pretty little rose of white flushed pink. Small flowers are very double against tiny light green leaves. One of the best of the miniatures, with dense and compact growth.
de Vink, Netherlands, 1953, continuous flowering, 12 x 10 in. (30 x 25 cm)

'Easter Morning'
Fully double flowers are creamy white with hints of lemon and are fragrant. Leaves are dark green providing a contrasting foil for the flowers. Growth is dense and inclined to be broad in habit. A good little rose.
Moore, USA, 1960, continuous flowering, 12 x 12 in. (30 x 30 cm)

'Hula Girl'
Pointed buds open to reveal double flowers of bright orange to salmon pink with just a touch of yellow at the base of the petals. Blooms are profuse over a long period on a plant with mid-green glossy foliage.
Williams, USA, 1975, continuous flowering, 12 x 12 in. (30 x 30 cm)

'June Time'
Flowers are mid-pink with a deeper pink reverse and are very double, borne in small clusters. Foliage is dark and glossy and reasonably resistant to disease. Growth is dense and spreading thanks to the *Rosa wichuraiana* influence in its parentage.
Moore, USA, 1963, continuous flowering, 12 x 12 in. (30 x 30 cm)

Shrub Roses

There are very many shrub roses all of differing nature, there are summer-flowering varieties and those that flower well into the autumn. Some set hips, some double as small climbers, some will be content to remain at knee height, and others will grow above the height of any person. Colors vary from white to deep purple, some have single flowers, while others are very, very double, some are scented and some not. So on it goes. Shrub roses are, between themselves, individual but within their groups they share similarities, both in habit and flower form, and although the group to which they belong is not the ultimate factor in choosing one variety against another, the characteristics of each group will, if understood, aid in the decision. Their use is diverse from mixed and specimen planting to growing in tubs.

'Alba Maxima' has typical green-gray alba foliage.

Albas

Dating back to the 15th century, the albas are one of the oldest "families" of the rose available today. They have characteristic gray-green leaves and pastel shaded flowers, the deepest coloring being mid silvery pink and they are refined in their beauty. They are highly perfumed and bloom en masse in midsummer. They are a very healthy bunch, matt leaves seeming to deter the unwanted spores of disease. 'Alba Maxima' with its double white flowers is said by some to be the White Rose Of York adopted by Edward Duke of York, later to be Edward IV, as the symbol of his house on defeating the Lancastrians at Mortimer's Cross in 1461. It was an alba rose 'Maiden's Blush' that caught the attention of my father as a child and stimulated his interest in roses, a genus which would go on to become his life's preoccupation. Without his inspiration it is possible that I never would have appreciated the rose.

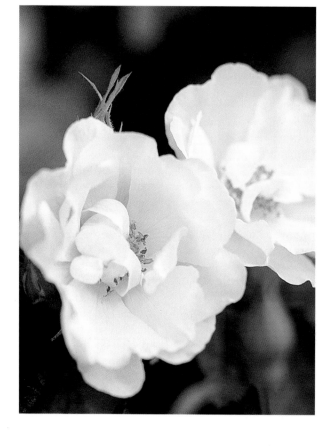

'Alba Semi-Plena' produces hips in autumn.

'Alba Maxima'

Also known as 'Jacobite Rose' and 'White Rose of York.' This rose is one of the candidates put forward as being the 'White Rose of York,' although expert opinion suggests that this was actually *Rosa alba*. Double, in-furled flowers are white, occasionally flushed with cream or, when grown in shade, blush pink, with a lovely refined perfume. They appear in clusters against very deep gray green leaves and thorny upright stems. Will sometime set hips that are ovoid in shape.
15th century or before, summer flowering, 6 x 4 ft. (1.8 x 1.2 m)

'Alba Semi-plena'

Semidouble flowers are pure white, slightly cupped, have a coronet of bright golden anthers, and are sweetly scented. Foliage is dark gray green and matt. This Alba will produce a good display of hips in the autumn.
Of unknown origin, likely to be 16th century or before, summer flowering, 8 x 5 ft. (2.5 x 1.5 m)

'Celestial'

This is a beautiful rose with saucer-shaped semidouble soft pink blooms, also known as 'Celeste.' These are scented and dominate the plant in profusion for two or three weeks in summer. Their brief appearance is complimented by soft gray-green leaves that make up for their absence later in the season. The perfume exuded by the flowers is strong yet unpretentious. A good rose as far as growth habit and disease resistance are concerned.
Of unknown origin very old, summer flowering, 6 x 4 ft. (1.8 x 1.2 m)

'Königin von Dänemark'

Also known as ' Queen of Denmark,' this variety has perhaps the deepest coloring of the albas, being rich to silvery pink. The flowers which are perhaps a little smaller than that of its relations are heavily scented and fully double. Leaves although of similar coloring are tougher in appearance.
Booth, Denmark, 1826, summer flowering, 5 x 4 ft. (1.5 x 1.2 m)

'Mme. Legras de St Germain'

Flowers are a little smaller than the majority of albas, creamy white, and perfumed and produced abundantly in clusters. Foliage is soft gray-green with few thorns. This is a vigorous member of its group and, if grown on a wall, will attain greater height than if it is grown as a free-standing shrub.
Early 19th century, summer flowering, 7 x 6 ft. (2.1 x 1.8 m)

'Maiden's Blush Great'

This is a beautiful rose with wonderfully perfumed blush pink, double flowers and soft gray-green leaves that clothe the plant when flowering is over. In France, it is known as 'Cuisse de Nymphe' or *Nymph's thigh*, but this was too much for the Victorians in England who renamed it.
Of unknown origin, likely to date from the 15th century or earlier, summer flowering 6 x 5 ft. (1.8 x 1.5 m)

Bourbons

The Bourbons take their name from an island in the southern Indian Ocean, Île de Bourbon (now called Réunion). In habit, this is a varying group, from shrubs of around a yard through to larger shrubs which are suitable as small climbers with support, to vigorous climbers. (The climbers are described later on.) Flowers, in many shades from white to deep purple-reds, are usually perfumed some of them very strongly, and are generally double in formation. Most repeat or continue to flower throughout the summer months and often into autumn. There are some excellent and some very famous varieties to be found among the ranks of the Bourbons.

'Boule de Neige'

French for *snowball*, the name reveals that the white petals of this lovely flower reflex to form a globular flower. Sometimes tinged with a purplish red when in bud, they are highly scented. Leaves are dark and glossy. Repeats well in the right situation.
Lacharme, France, 1867, repeat flowering, 4 x 3 ft. (1.2 x 1 m)

'Commandant Beaurepaire'

An elegant striped variety with large flowers streaked and marbled with pink, white and purple, scented and with golden anthers at their centers. Leaves are long and pointed, mid-green in color. 'Commandant Beaurepaire' will tolerate some shade where its unusual coloring will be most resplendent. A good rose, well worth considering if a striped rose is desired.
Moreau-Robert, France, 1874, repeat flowering, 5 x 5 ft. (1.5 x 1.5 m)

'Gipsy Boy'

This is a lax shrub rose that can also double as a climber. Flowers are not huge but double, crimson-purple and scented putting on a mass display in season. Slightly wrinkled mid-green leaves clothe the shrub amply. This is a vigorous rose producing new canes of growth throughout the summer. Often sets hips.
Lambert, Germany, 1909, summer flowering, 6 x 4 ft. (1.8 x 1.2 m)

'Louise Odier'

An excellent rose. From round tight buds emerge highly scented, fully double, cupped flowers of mid-silvery pink. As they mature they become flatter, exposing the anthers, and slightly ragged inner petals that are often tinged with lilac. With regular deadheading flowers will be produced regularly throughout the summer. Arching growth can be encouraged to climb when this variety is grown near a wall.
Margottin, France, 1851, continuous flowering, 5 x 4 ft. (1.5 x 1.2 m)

Opposite 'Mme. Isaac Pereire' has an outstanding perfume.

'Mme. Isaac Pereire'

The color of the huge blowsy blooms of 'Mme. Isaac Pereire' is best described as purplish pink, which fades in hot sun. The perfume they emit is heady and powerful. Long arching canes of growth make it well-suited to climbing, as the heavy blooms are inclined to nod down they can be better appreciated if higher up. Early blooms are sometimes prone to proliferation but there will be many more to follow so this should not be considered too much of a draw back. Leaves are large, pointed, and maroon edged.
Garçon, France, 1881, continuous flowering, 7 x 5 ft. (2.1 x 1.5 m)

'Mme. Pierre Oger'

Like the rose from which it sported, 'La Reine Victoria,' this also has cupped double blooms borne in clusters that remain globular for much of their life. They are soft delicate pink with the color intensified in shade, and highly perfumed. This is a rose of superior form and beauty and for this it is very popular. Leaves are pointed, mid-green and, sadly, rather prone to disease later in the season, but this should not be a deter you from choosing it if you spray for such problems.
Verdier, France, 1878, continuous flowering, 4 x 4 ft. (1.2 x 1.2 m)

'Souvenir de la Malmaison'

This is a truly beautiful rose with large, flat, quartered blooms of soft blush pink that exude a wonderful perfume. They appear repeatedly throughout the summer on a strongly growing plant. Its only drawback is a tendency to ball in wet weather but, if one has the time, the outer shell of petals can be carefully teased open to allow the flower to emerge naturally. It is said that in 1814 Empress Josephine handed a bloom of a rose to Tzar Alexander, Emperor of Russia, saying as she did so "Un souvenir de la Malmaison." Later when visiting France, the Grand Duke of Russia recalled these words and suggested that the name be given to a seedling rose sent to Malmaison by the breeder Beluze and this lovely rose is it.
Beluze, France, 1943, continuous flowering, 6 x 6 ft. (1.8 x 1.8 m)

Centifolias

Also known as provence roses or cabbage roses. centifolias are the "roses of a hundred petals" and date from the 15th and 16th centuries. They are the large blowsy-bloomed roses, (hence their other name of cabbage roses), so often portrayed in the paintings of the Old Masters, which is understandable as it was the Dutch breeders of that era that carried out much pioneering work in the introduction of new varieties. Some of them can be difficult to situate in the garden, as they are a little cumbersome in growth. If you have the space to cope with long, arching branches, the larger varieties will reward you with abundant, beautiful shaggy, highly perfumed blooms but they will require some support. The smaller centifolias, however, are often quite neat with flowers more in proportion with their size.

'Blanchefleur'

Flowers, which are a little smaller than some of its group, are white sometimes edged pink, double and open flat exuding a delightful scent. They appear in bunches in abundance. It is more compact than many of its relations, with gray-green soft foliage. It is tolerant of poor soils and will brighten a shaded place, which it will cope with reasonably well.
Vibert, France, 1835,
summer flowering
5 x 4 ft. (15 x 12 cm)

'Fantin Latour'

This is one of the most beautiful of the centifolias. Its flowers are full, flat, and quartered, soft powder pink with, in my opinion, a sumptuous perfume. It has attractive deepish green, rounded foliage and strong arching growth. Although clearly named for the famous artist, Henri Fantin Latour, little more is known of its origin.
Probably 19th century,
Summer flowering,
5 x 4 ft. (1.5 x 1.2 m)

'Rose de Meaux'

This is one of the tidiest and most compact-growing centifolias. Its growth is upright and short. Flowers are semidouble, cupped and in ratio to the size of the plant, soft to mid-pink. Leaves are also small, pointed and gray-green. A lovely little rose that is useful near the front of a border or in a tub.
Sweet, UK, prior to 1789,
summer flowering,
24 x 24 in. (60 x 60 cm)

'Tour de Malakoff'

Big blowsy flowers are bright magenta-pink when at their peak and fade slowly through shades of purple to lilac-gray. They have a super perfume. The plant itself is lax and vigorous and will often benefit from support. Sometimes called the 'Taffeta Rose.'
Soupert and Notting,
Luxembourg, 1856,
summer flowering,
5 x 4 ft. (1.5 x 1.2 m)

'White Provence'

Also known as 'Unique Blanche.' The growth of this rose can often be unruly but, although they hate wet weather, the flowers can truly compensate. Creamy white with a sheen to the petals, they appear slightly later than many once-flowering varieties and give away a lovely perfume; this is a true connoisseur's variety.
First found in UK in 1775,
summer flowering,
5 x 4 ft. 91.5 x 1.2 m)

Opposite: Cécile Brunner has clusters of dainty flowers (shown twice normal size).

Chinas

As their name suggests, these roses originally derived from China, where it is believed that they existed as far back as the 10th century, even before. They are important in the history of the rose as they are largely responsible for the long flowering period of most of today's modern roses. They cover a wide palette of color and range of habits and many of them are perfumed. Their use is diverse, suited to bedding, specimen, or container planting but they are not on the whole hardy roses and may need protection in colder areas during the winter months. They are rewarding cool greenhouse or conservatory plants.

'Cécile Brunner'

Also known as 'Sweetheart Rose.' The individual flowers are not huge and stunning, more elegant and delicate but when blooming en masse they are collectively lovely. Small, shell pink and pointed in bud, they open in a slightly ragged style on the end of long stems in clusters. The long flower stem makes them ideal for button holes. The plant is not overly endowed with foliage, individual leaves are slender, and growth is a little awkward. Having said this, 'Cécile Brunner' is a good all-round rose. There are also white and climbing forms available. *Pernet Ducher, France, 1881, continuous flowering, 4 x 2 ft. (1.2 m x 60 cm)*

'Old Blush'

Also known as 'Parson's Pink.' An important rose in that, very early on, it was used in breeding programs and is largely the reason for the remontant qualities in today's hybrids. It was discovered growing in China and had reached Europe by the 1780s. It is still worthy of inclusion in the garden today. Semi-double open flowers are mid-silvery pink and scented. A large shrub rose that can be grown as a climber if given some support. *Parson, China, continuous flowering, 6 x 4 ft. (1.8 x 1.2 m)*

Mutabilis

This must be one of the most characteristically individual roses. Single flowers, when fresh, are a blend of many shades including apricot, yellow, orange, pink, and red, almost invariably with age settling on a shade of raspberry pink. This may sound peculiar but the effect is quite stunning, and this rose has to be one of my favorites, not for its uniqueness, although this has some relevance but because it is a truly fantastic sight. Young growth is plum colored, which adds to its crazy palette. In some situations it will remain relatively dwarf, in others it will do its best to climb.
China, 1932,
continuous flowering,
4 x 3 ft. (1.2 x 1 m)

'Perle d'Or'

Very much like 'Cécile Brunner,' although I prefer the coloring of this being buff to apricot with pink tinges. Flowers are held on long stems in clusters. Growth is a little less angular but still somewhat awkward, a typical China trait. Stems are almost thorn free and foliage is dark. 'Perle d'Or' enjoys good conditions and in the most favorable' it will get taller than the size stated here.
Dubreuil, France, 1884,
continuous flowering,
4 x 2 ft. (1.2 m x 60 cm)

'Sophie's Perpetual'

I hesitated in including this variety in the shrub section of this directory, but have settled on doing so, as it will only attain useful climbing size in very good conditions. Having said this, be prepared for it to outgrow the suggested size once its roots find welcoming soil. I am a fan of this rose which, while perhaps not possessing the most beautiful of flowers, has a lovely perfume and is generally healthy. Individually the flowers are double, faint pink and heavily edged with cherry cerise. This is a free-flowering clustered variety.
Re-introduced in 1960, UK,
continuous flowering,
8 x 4 ft. (2.5 x 1.2 m)

'Viridiflora'

Also known as 'Green Rose.' I could not leave this variety out as it is such a peculiarity. Blooms are almost deformed, with normal petals replaced by green, brown tinged bracts, that become purplish brown as they mature. This is a rose for the collector or flower arranger with a sense of humor. Generally healthy and easy to grow.
Of unknown origin,
but around 1833,
continuous flowering,
3 x 3 ft. (1 x 1 m)

Damasks

The damasks are known to have been around in Roman and Ancient Greek times. In the Middle East they were prized for their scent and were used for the extraction of attar or oil of roses to produce perfume. The exact timing of their arrival in Europe is unknown but they have been here for many, many years. Although not a huge number of them exist, they are beautiful roses, ranging from mid-pink to white in color and are generally scented. Most flower just once but there are one or two exceptions, in particular 'Quatre Saisons' which has a good second flush of flowers. In fact it was this rose that allowed the Roman pagan festival of Rosalia, which was held first in early summer to be repeated in early autumn. They are a robust group of roses which are probably best placed in the rose or mixed shrubbery.

'Ispahan'

'Quatre Saisons' is typical of the damasks famed for their perfume.

This rose flowers for a long season. The very fragrant flowers are double and well shaped with reflexed petals, unfading mid- to soft pink. The shrub is strong in growth with mid green leaves and is relatively free of thorns.
Middle East, probably Persia, prior to 1832, summer flowering,
4 x 3 ft. (1.2 x 1 m)

'Kazanlik'

Bearing the name of one of the centers of the perfume industry in the Middle East of its time, this is a wonderful, deliciously perfumed damask rose. Slightly shaggy, double to semidouble flowers are warm mid-pink, fading just a little as they age. A good shrub specimen that may need some support in the garden.
Middle East, date of origin unknown, summer flowering, 5 x 4 ft. (1.5 x 1.2 m)

'Léda'

Also known as 'Painted Damask.' It is clear to see why this rose has been given its second name, for its pure white flowers are edged with crimson, almost as though someone had painstakingly touched them up with a brush and paint. Individually the flowers have reflexed outer petals and infurled central ones, giving them a rounded shape. They are scented and borne on a tidy, generally healthy plant.
Probably early 19th century, summer flowering, 5 x 3 ft. (1.5 x 1 m)

'Mme. Hardy'

A famous old variety. White flowers are double and of good size, exposing at their centers a distinctive green eye, and are scented. Once settled this rose can produce a good number of exquisite blooms, almost obliterating its foliage. Strong growth is relatively tidy and produces bright green, somewhat glossy foliage
Hardy, France, 1832, summer flowering, 5 x 5 ft. (1.5 x 1.5 m)

'Mme. Hardy' has a significant green eye at the center of the flower.

'Quatre Saisons'

Also known as 'Autumn Damask.' The flowers appear unusually, for this group, in two flushes on this magnificent plant. They are mid- to soft pink, double, ragged in formation and highly scented. A good candidate for the making of potpourri. An unkempt plant in many ways, it produces early autumn flowers on the growth had in the summer of the same year, which must be borne in mind during any pruning.
Middle East, very old, summer flowering, 4 x 3 ft. (1.2 x 1 m)

Gallicas

The crusaders of the 12th and 13th centuries brought specimens and seeds of roses from the east to Europe and it is likely that many of these were gallicas. During the Middle Ages, the chemists of the time used many roses in the treatment of various ailments and the famous, *Rosa gallica officinallis* was one of the varieties they most frequently depended on, in fact it is often listed today as the 'Apothecary's Rose.' It is also the Red Rose of Lancaster adopted by Henry IV as the symbol of his house and made famous due to the Wars of the Roses. Later, these roses found favor with the Empress Josephine who is said to have collected more than 150 varieties at her garden at the Château Malmaison. In habit they are strong growing and tough, most of them are perfumed, and in color they range from soft shades of pink to deep purples and maroons. The flowers are diverse in shape, anything from single to large and fully double. On the whole they are tidy and not too well endowed with thorns. They are usually tolerant of poor soil and shade, flowering in great abundance in midsummer, they are at home almost anywhere. When grown on their own roots, gallicas will sucker freely. There are some beautiful members of this group, and no rose garden is complete with out at least one.

Opposite: 'Rosa mundi' dates back to the 12th century.

'Belle de Crécy'
Medium-sized flowers are lilac-purple, fading to gray as they mature. Although this coloris different to the majority of roses, there are some of similar coloring that surpass this one, but it is easier to place in the garden than some of these due to its reasonable size. Having said this, when the weather is good, so are the flowers and they are well scented. Growth is upright and almost free of thorns.
Hardy, France, 1829, summer flowering, 4 x 3 ft. (1.2 x 1 m)

'Cardinal de Richelieu'
From tight buds of magenta-red emerge fully double flowers of rich purple. The central petals are furled inward, demonstrating their lighter reverse and hiding the stamens. They are deliciously perfumed and are held in clusters. The foliage is silky and dark green, often when young edged with maroon. Not many thorns at all.
Laffay, France, around 1840, summer flowering, 4 x 3 ft. (1.2 x 1 m)

'Charles de Mills'
This is a famous old cultivar and everyone's favorite when in full flush. The large blooms when open are broad mushroom shaped and almost perfectly round, consisting of very many petals. In color they are a mixture of maroon and purple, overall somewhere between the two. I find this rose heavily scented but others find it almost devoid of perfume. Foliage is dark on smooth stems.
Of unknown origin, an old variety, summer flowering, 4 x 4 ft. (1.2 x 1.2 m)

'Duchesse de Montebello'
A beautiful rose. Flowers are fully double, soft, clear and bright pink with a sweet perfume. Inner petals furl inward around a bright green eye and, when open, they are the shape of a shallow dish. Foliage is relatively healthy and dark, new growth is lavish and almost cane like. 'Duchesse de Montebello' will tolerate poor soils and shade to some extent.
Laffay, France, 1829, summer flowering, 4 x 3 ft. (1.2 x 1 m)

'Empress Josephine'
Named in honor of the Empress, this is a truly lovely rose. Wavy petals make up the slightly ragged flowers which are, in essence, deep pink, but heavy veining and tinges of blush and occasionally lilac give them a softer appearance. They are scented. A somewhat lax grower yet well foliated. Generally tolerant of all but the worst conditions.
Of unknown origin, though to be early 19th century, summer flowering, 5 x 4 ft. (1.5 x 1.2 m)

'James Mason'
A relatively recent addition to the gallicas, this is a stunning rose, created by my father. When breeding it he relied on the red coloring and health of 'Scharlachglut,' a shrub/climbing rose of the 1950s and the qualities of the superb 'Tuscany Superb' to supply its offspring with the best of both parents, and this they did. The flowers are abundant in midsummer, semi-single, carmine-red, with a velvety sheen and a bold coronet of bright golden anthers. They are large, lightly scented and slightly cupped with the odd petal reflexing backward. Foliage is dark and leathery, clothing the plant well.
Beales, UK, 1982, summer flowering, 5 x 4 ft. (1.5 x 1.2 m)

'Tuscany Superb'
I had to include this beautiful rose. Flowers are medium in size, semi-double and possess a very heady fragrance. In colorthey are rich purple-red, and velvety both in sheen and to the touch, open and flat, they display contrasting golden anthers. Foliage is dark green and generally healthy, growth upright.
Paul, UK, 1848, summer flowering, 4 x 3 ft. (1.2 x 1 m)

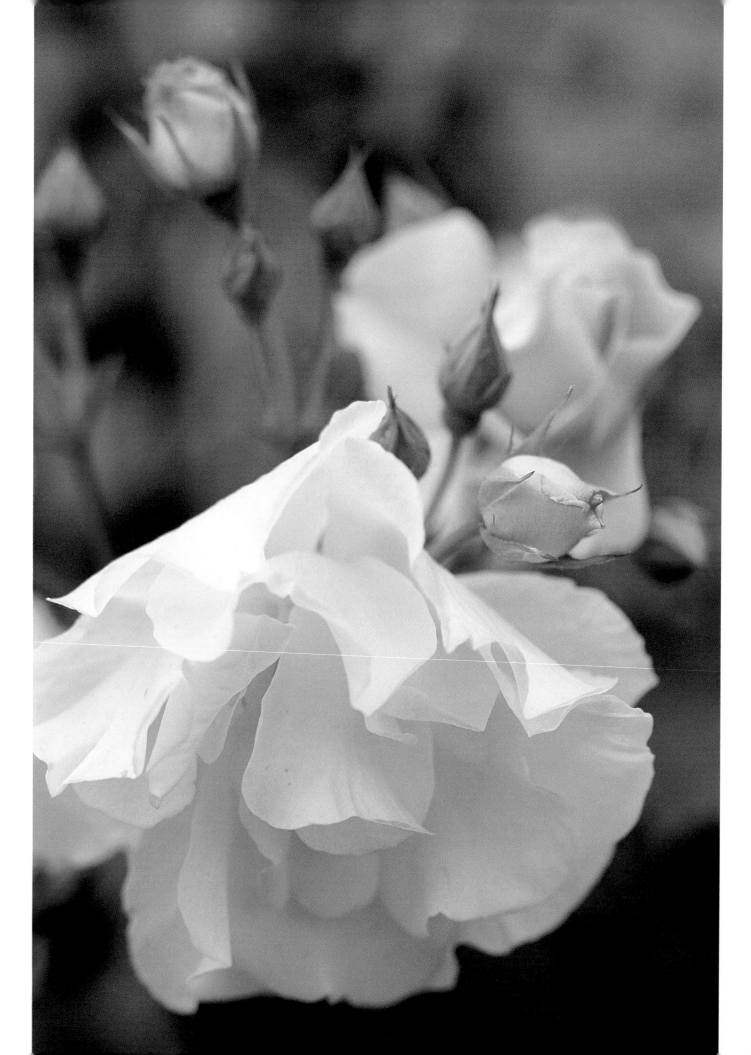

Hybrid Musks

These were the first tidy, continuous-flowering shrub roses, originally classified as hybrid teas and then called Pemberton roses after the Rev. Joseph Pemberton who bred them between 1913 and 1926. He bred some excellent varieties that are still popular today. The majority of hybrid musks were created by Pemberton, but a few were introduced after his death and many of these are still with us also. Although the majority produce their blooms in clusters, individually they vary in color and form, from creamy white single blooms to flamboyant red and fully double. Most are scented. They are useful garden plants, the smaller varieties adapt well to growing in tubs while some of the taller varieties can be persuaded to grow as small climbers when positioned against a wall. Most will even suffer shade and poor soil.

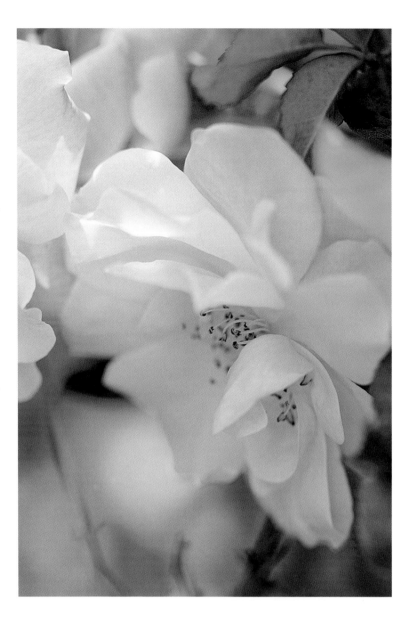

'Ballerina'

This is an outstanding rose, and one of the most popular garden roses today. Flowers are small and single in large clusters, pink with white centers. They appear continuously, especially if the plant is regularly deadheaded, through the summer and into the autumn. Leaves are narrow and plentiful. 'Ballerina' is excellent when grown in a tub. *Bentall, UK, 1937, continuous flowering, 4 x 3 ft. (1.2 x 1 m)*

'Buff Beauty'

The flowers of this variety seem to vary in color from one garden to another, from soft buff to bright apricot-orange, largely due to the soil and amount of sun on them. They are double, scented, and appear in clusters.

Leaves are dark green and glossy. The growth can be vigorous and spreading, allowing this rose to be grown as a small climber with support if desired. *Bentall, UK, 1939, continuous flowering, 5 x 5 ft. (1.5 x 1.5 m)*

'Felicia'

One of the most lovely hybrid musks. Medium-sized, double flowers are soft pink with hints of salmon and are nicely scented. Slightly deeper blooms appear in early autumn. A plant of reasonable vigor and health with dark, slightly crinkled foliage. *Pemberton, UK, 1928, continuous flowering, 4 x 4 ft. (1.2 x 1.2 m)*

Above: Felicia is very free flowering.

Opposite: The flowers of 'Penelope' open flat from peachy pink buds.

'Moonlight'

Small flowers are semi-single, creamy white, with a tinge of yellow and golden stamens; they are borne in large clusters of buds and open blooms. Foliage is dark and healthy, a contrasting foil to the blooms. This variety is particularly good in the autumn when the yellow shading of the flowers is more prominent. *Pemberton, UK, 1913, continuous flowering 5 x 4 ft. (1.5 x 1.2 m)*

'Penelope'

Flowers are large and semidouble, with frilled petals of cream tinged soft pink, they open flat to reveal prominent golden stamens and are delightfully scented. Foliage is dark and growth upright. With regular deadheading 'Penelope' will flower well into the autumn. *Pemberton, UK, 1924, continuous flowering, 5 x 4 ft. (1.5 x 1.2 m)*

Hybrid Perpetuals

The name of this group is a little misleading as they are not totally perpetual, although they will usually supply at least one second flush of flower each year. Most were bred in the early part of the 1800s and are the forerunners of the hybrid teas. The hybrid perpetuals were very popular with the Victorians who loved their big sumptuous blooms. Plants vary in size from tidy compact shrubs to those with more vigorous arching growth but, in nearly every case, the flowers are scented, often powerfully. Best grown as companions to other roses or shrubs.

Right: 'Ferdinand Pichard' is a focal point in any garden.

Below: 'Baronne Prévost' has large, very double strongly perfumed flowers.

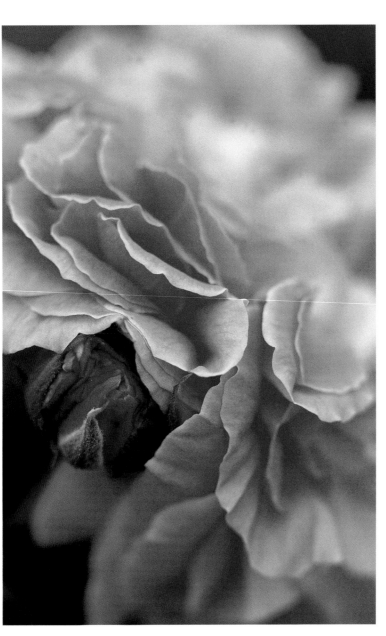

'Baroness Rothschild'

This is a superior rose with very large, full, and cupped flowers of clear rose pink with a silky texture to the petals. They are held erect on strong stems above abundant mid-green leaves. Growth too is upright on a medium-sized shrub.
Pernet Père, France, 1868, repeat flowering, 4 x 3 ft. (1.2 x 1 m)

'Baronne Prévost'

Very double blooms comprising many petals are strong rose pink and perfumed. They appear abundantly for the first flush of flowers, but not quite as heavily later on. Growth can be a little willowy but bushy with dark leaves and many vicious thorns. An attractive rose that is best placed toward the back of the border.
Desprez, France, 1842, repeat flowering, 5 x 4 ft. (1.5 x 1.2 m)

'Éclair'

Very dark red, almost black, velvety petals form fully double, very attractive and scented flowers. Growth is upright and prickly, but can be a little sparse when it comes to foliage. A rose that needs a good spot in the garden, growing best in well nourished soil.
Lacharme, France, 1833, repeat flowering, 4 x 3 ft. (1.2 x 1 m)

'Ferdinand Pichard'

Stripes of carmine stand out boldly against a pinky-white background color on the petals of double, well-scented flowers. They appear repeatedly throughout summer on a vigorous shrub, which sends out long arms of new growth. Leaves are large and pointed.
Tanne, France, 1921, repeat flowering, 5 x 4 ft. (1.5 x 1.2 m)

'Reine des Violettes'

Large double flowers are soft violet to lilac in shade, paling as they age to a lilac-gray and emit a lovely perfume. They are flat, quartered, and petals furl in at the center. Leaves are a gray-green, not at all coarse and stems are relatively smooth. This is an excellent rose for the garden, and will even grow well in a tub.
Millet-Malet, France, 1860, continuous flowering, 5 x 3 ft. (1.5 x 1m)

Modern Shrub Roses and the New English Roses

The modern shrub roses are a group consisting of roses of relatively recent introduction, called such because they are of mixed parentage, making them difficult to place elsewhere because there is not a particular group with which any they have strong affinity. They are a diverse group with flowers in different colors, styles, and sizes. Some are scented, some not very much. Most grow to above a yard and some can be adapted to climb in the right situation. The majority are relatively healthy but there are some that need coddling to get the best from them and others that will withstand poor situations. This is, as you may imagine, a huge group so I have had to be very selective in choosing the varieties described below.

New English roses are also a group of mixed progeny; their name having been adopted for marketing purposes rather than for any other reason but these days the word "new" is generally dropped. In reality they are simply modern shrub roses. They are actually a combination of old roses, to which they owe their appearance and new roses, hybrid teas, and floribundas mainly, which provide the "English roses" with their remontancy. Most of them are strong growing, with the occasional tendency to be a little lax and willowy; some are even suitable for use as small climbers. Although there are a few with an annoying tendency to pick up disease, most are healthy but this is the case with all roses. Their use in the garden is varied; the shorter, bushier varieties are good in a tub and equally at home in the shrubbery, which is the best place for larger specimens. They all seem to benefit from a good prune to keep them within bounds and to prevent them from becoming top heavy. They all require regular deadheading to perpetuate blooming.

'Henry Kelsey' is a rudely healthy shrub rose.

'Cuthbert Grant'

The individual flowers of this variety are semidouble, deep velvety red with a proud circle of golden anthers but it is more the combined effect of very many blooms that is stunning. A healthy rose with glossy leaves and bushy vigorous growth.
Canadian Department of Agriculture, 1967, repeat flowering, 4 x 3 ft. (1.2 x 1 m)

'Graham Thomas'

This must rank as one of the best of the English roses. Flowers are rich yellow, paling with age, cupped in shape, double and with a heady perfume. They appear in clusters on a willowy plant with dark to mid-green, glossy leaves.
English rose, Austin, UK, 1983, continuous flowering, 4 x 3 ft. (1.2 x 1 m)

'Jacqueline du Pré'

A super shrub rose with much to recommend it. Ivory-cream blooms are semisingle in clusters with prominent pink to gold stamens; they are shaped very much like a water lily and have a musk-like perfume. Plump buds are buff to apricot. The foliage is dark and glossy.
Harkness, UK, 1989, repeat flowering, 4 x 5 ft. (1.2 x 1.5 m)

'Lichtkönigin Lucia'

This is a very useful and healthy shrub rose. Semidouble flowers are bright yellow are scented and appear in clusters. Growth is upright yet bushy with mid- to bright green, glossy foliage. There are few yellow shrub roses with the attributes of this one.
Kordes, Germany, 1966, continuous flowering, 4 x 3 ft. (1.2 x 1 m)

'Macmillan Nurse'

The blooms that emerge from plump buds are very double, almost quartered, white with a hint of peach at the base of the petals. They are borne in clusters on a healthy, strong-growing plant with dark glossy leaves and well armed branches. As one bloom falls so another appears, all summer long.
Beales, UK, 1998, continuous flowering, 3 x 3 ft. (1 x 1 m)

'Mary Rose'

Rich rose pink, scented blooms are old fashioned in style being slightly cupped and very double, deeper pink at the center. They are borne in clusters on the end of long and arching shoots. Foliage is glossy and dark and growth dense and open in habit.
English rose, Austin, UK, 1983, continuous flowering, 4 x 3 ft. (1.2 x 1 m)

'Raymond Carver'

An excellent rose bred by Colin Horner but introduced to the market place by my father. Blooms are amber to apricot with buff undertones. They are very double, almost crinkled and are delightfully scented in clusters on the end of strong, straight stems. Leaves are large, dark and when young, copper tinged. Will tolerate poor soils.
Beales, UK, 1999, continuous flowering, 4 x 3 ft. (1.2 x 1 m)

'Sadler's Wells'

This variety is outstanding in the autumn when many other roses have since finished blooming; it is good earlier on also. Flowers are semisingle, silvery pink, heavily edged with cherry red. They appear in clusters of around five or six

blooms on the end of long, strong and upright shoots. Leaves are dark and glossy. A good rose for cutting.
Beales, UK, 1983, continuous flowering, 4 x 3 ft. (1.2 x 1 m)

'Westerland'

Although a little bright for my taste, this is a good all-rounder. Blooms are apricot to orange, large and a little shaggy with some scent and they appear regularly throughout the summer. It is very vigorous and upright in habit with large mid- to dark green leaves. Tolerant of poorer situations.
Kordes, Germany, 1969, continuous flowering, 4 x 3 ft. (1.2 x 1 m)

Above: 'Macmillan Nurse' is very healthy and free flowering.

Opposite: 'Raymond Carver' can not be beaten for its quantity of blooms and healthy disposition.

Moss roses

This is a fascinating family of roses, for it is perhaps not the flowers that are the most appealing features, but the stems and unopened buds. They are endowed with moss-like glands, some varieties more than others, which, when touched, have a wonderful balsam-like fragrance. These roses are separately classified as moss roses, but this group really belongs to the centifolias. It was a sport of *Rosa centifolia* called *R. centifolia muscosa* that first appeared early in the 19th century, and was used extensively in breeding programs through which new varieties with moss-like glands were created. Some have masses of soft moss, and there are some with little more than high density thorns. I am sure that if they were not so novel there would be many in this group that would have become extinct, but every rose has its place and among the ranks of the moss roses are some excellent varieties.

'Alfred de Dalmas'

Although possibly related to the Portland damasks, it warrants inclusion in this group because of its mossed stems. Blooms are semidouble, shell pink, cupped and scented. Unusually for a moss they appear reasonably continuously throughout the summer on a tidy plant with plentiful foliage.
A good rose with several uses in the garden, not least of which is its suitability for growing in a tub.
Portemer, France, 1855, continuous flowering, 3 x 2 ft. (1 m x 60 cm)

'Chapeau de Napoléon'

The full, double, highly scented flowers of this rose are delightful, but not the reason for its popularity. The flower buds are heavily endowed with moss to the extent that they form a shape similar to that of a cocked hat. The resemblance is uncanny. Whatever its novelty value, this is a good shrub worthy of inclusion in the garden, although it can be a little lax in habit.
Vibert, France, 1826, summer flowering, 5 x 4 ft. (1.5 x 1.2 m)

Pimpinellifolias or Scotch Briars

Also known as burnets, this little group of very hardy roses is native to Europe. In form they are very prickly, compact, and their foliage consists of many tiny serrated leaflets. The flowers are generally small, appearing in abundance in early summer and usually followed by a display of shiny rotund mahogany-colored hips later in the year. They will grow almost anywhere, in a cool, shaded aspect, in poor soil and will cope with the worst winters, hence their second name, Scotch briars. Robert Brown, of Perth Scotland, found a Scotch rose growing wild in the hills near Perth. He gathered the seed and it was sown at the nursery of Dickson & Brown in Perth in 1793. The seeds produced a double rose and, in time, variations of it were grown. The numbers of these little roses increased until, it is said, another Scottish grower had more than one hundred varieties. English growers soon became aware of them, and their popularity spread. Today many of these are lost, but we still have a good selection of them, and many newer hybrids to choose from. Their density and thorny disposition makes them ideal candidates for the shorter boundary hedge, where sharp thorns will provide a good deterrent.

'Common Moss'

Also known as 'Old Pink Moss.' Probably a version of *Rosa centifolia muscosa*, of which it seems there are several. Flowers are mid-rose pink, double, and highly perfumed. Well mossed with ample, slightly crinkled foliage. A good moss rose which is perhaps most at home toward the back of the border.
France, pre-1700, summer flowering, 4 x 4 ft. (1.2 x 1.2 m)

'Nuits de Young'

Smallish flowers are purple to deep red, a color which is intensified by contrasting golden anthers. Leaves are not large and moss is not overwhelming but the color of the flowers is eye-catching, a good focal point in among roses of other shades.
Laffay, France, 1845, summer flowering, 4 x 3 ft. (1.2 x 1 m)

'William Lobb'

A very vigorous variety with long, arching canes of new growth. Flowers are borne in clusters and are a mixture of purple, lilac, and gray, sometimes with a hint of pink. They are double and lightly scented. Can be grown as a small climber but may require some support even when encouraged to grow as a shrub.
Laffay, France, 1855, summer flowering, 8 x 5 ft. (2.5 x 1.5 m)

'Burnet Double White'

Flowers are cupped, semi-double and dainty with bright golden anthers. The are produced abundantly on small shrubs with masses of tiny serrated leaves. In the autumn the flowers are replaced by small round, dark and polished mahogany, almost black, hips. There are also pink and marbled pink versions named respectively 'Burnet Double Pink' and 'Burnet Marbled Pink.'
Uncertain origin, pre-1650, spring or early summer flowering 3 x 3 ft. (1 x 1 m)

'Frühlingsduft'

There are a number of 'Frühlings' hybrids, all remarkably hardy and all bred by Kordes of Germany, but this has to be my favorite of them all. Flowers are fully double, creamy yellow with buff to pink tinges at their centers. Foliage is tough, slightly crinkled, glossy and dark green. A good rose but it does require space.
Kordes, Germany, 1949, summer flowering, 10 x 6 ft. (3 x 1.8 m)

'Maigold'

A hybrid pimpinellifolia that is best grown as a climber, although it will grow in the shrubbery if given some support. Blooms are semidouble apricot-orange blending toward yellow at the center. They are to my taste, bright but not gaudy and have a superb cupped shape. Borne in clusters early in the year, with the odd repeating bloom, amidst the most healthy dark green glossy foliage. If there is a draw back to this variety, it is the huge number of nasty thorns it possesses.
Kordes, Germany 1953
spring or early summer
flowering
12 x 8 ft. (3.8 x 2.5 m)

'Mary Queen of Scots'

An early-flowering variety that leaves you craving for further summer blooms. Flowers are single, creamy pink tinged deeper lilac-pink, with prominent stamens. Leaves are tiny and there are masses of them on plum to mahogany-colored wood. Hips follow the flowers and are round, deep maroon, almost black. A beautiful rose even if its blooms are short lived.
Of uncertain origin,
but very old,
spring or early summer
flowering,
3 x 3 ft. (1 x 1 m)

Above: 'Maigold' has many nasty prickles but is a healthy useful climber.

Right: 'The Fairy' has nodding clusters of bloom.

Polyanthas

These little roses were very popular in the early 20th century; they are small-flowered, low-growing roses with many uses. Their habit allows them to be easily grown in pots on the patio or balcony, and they make good edging to beds and borders as well as being free flowering and low growing enough for bedding. Flowers tend to be small, in clusters, and appear freely over a long period. Regular deadheading is important to extend flowering. Many of the polyanthas have sported from others and it is not uncommon to find a stem that has reverted to the parent plant. The polyanthas are often listed with floribundas, but their growth habit is somewhat different, they tend to be shorter, a little more prostrate, and produce larger trusses of smaller flowers.

'Baby Faurax'

The distinct violet coloring of the flowers of this little rose means that it stands out among other roses in this group. They are double, cupped, and held in large clusters, with streaks of white around prominent stamens. Growth is bushy, low, and slightly spreading.
Lille, France, 1924,
continuous flowering,
12 x 12 in. (30 x 30 cm)

'Cameo'

Small flowers are held in large bunches. They are soft salmon to flesh pink, cupped in shape, revealing golden anthers when fully open. Growth is bushy and well clothed with narrow, pointed, light green leaves. Thorns on older wood are very vicious.
de Ruiter, Holland, 1932,
continuous flowering,
24 x 24 in. (60 x 60 cm)

Portlands

Some of the most beautiful and easily managed old roses make up this small group. They are all at least repeat-flowering varieties and most give off expensive perfumes. They are neat and bushy in growth habit and are therefore excellent for smaller gardens. Their tidy proportions allow them to grow well in pots, and they also make good low hedging, and work well in formal group planting. Most of them will tolerate all but the very poorest of soil, but they do not favor too much shade. Their coloring ranges from white, through soft and mid pinks, to deep purple-reds.

Gloria Mundi
Large clusters of rich, scarlet-red flowers that are slightly cupped with white flecks at their centers. Growth is upright but bushy and clothed with many small dark leaves. Flowers freely into the autumn months, but may occasionally throw out a stem that has reverted to the rose from which it sported.
de Ruiter, Holland, 1929, continuous flowering, 24 x 24 in. (60 x 60 cm)

'Miss Edith Cavell'
This little rose disappeared for a while but was reintroduced by my father on the 70th anniversary of the execution of Nurse Edith Cavell by the Germans in World War I. At that time we lived in the village of her birth, and it was only after an appeal in the local paper by the Vicar of Swardeston that the rose was found again. Small rich red to scarlet, double flowers are borne in large clusters. Small leaves are dark green and plentiful.
de Ruiter, Holland, 1917, continuous flowering, 24 x 24 in. (60 x 60 cm)

'The Fairy'
The branches of this attractive rose grow in an arching manner which make it an interesting subject for a pot, where they will cascade outward. The blooms are small, soft pink and are bunched together in large clusters. Leaves are mid- to deep green and glossy, an attractive foil for the dainty blooms. Benefits from regular removal of the dead flower clusters.
Bentall, UK, 1932, continuous flowering, 2 x 4 ft. (60 cm x 1.2 m)

'Comte de Chambord' is a useful smaller proportioned shrub.

'Arthur de Sansal'
The beautiful flowers are crimson purple, very double and rosette-like in formation. They are highly perfumed and appear repeatedly throughout the flowering season. A neat, and bushy plant with large dark leaves. Unfortunately prone to mildew; probably not the best rose to include in an organic garden.
Cartier, France, 1847, repeat flowering, 3 x 2 ft. (1 m x 60 cm)

'Comte de Chambord'
Large, very double, flowers are rich glowing pink at the centers, where petals furl inward and softer pink toward the edge. They exude a strong and heady fragrance. Petals are delicate with a tissue-paper-like quality. The plant is not large but the leaves which are bright to gray-green are big.
Moreau-Robert, France, 1863, continuous flowering, 3 x 2 ft. (1 m x 60 cm)

'Duchess of Portland'
Also known as 'Portland Rose' this was the first rose of its type. Borne in small clusters, the flowers are semisingle, cerise with prominent stamens. Only slightly fragrant, they appear repeatedly throughout the summer. Foliage is mid- to light green and wood is prickly. Growth is tidy.
Introducer unknown, probably from Italy, around 1790, repeat flowering, 3 x 2 ft. (1 m x 60 cm)

'Jacques Cartier'
Flat blooms are soft mid-pink, and highly scented. Petals toward the center furl in, while those on the outer edges often furl away from the flower. They are held erect on strong stems amid leathery mid-green foliage. In the United States, 'Jacques Cartier' is sometimes sold as 'Marquise Boccella.'
Moreau-Robert, France, 1686, continuous flowering, 3 x 2 ft. (1 m x 60 cm)

Procumbents

"Ground cover" is a commonly used term in the garden, but there are few roses that truly cover the ground. At our nursery, we prefer to call them procumbent roses, which more readily describes their arching, wide-growing habit. There are many ways of growing them, from hiding eyesores such as manhole covers, to spilling down banks or tumbling over walls, and some will even be happy in hanging baskets. In the right position, when against a wall for example, they can be encouraged to climb and the more vigorous of them will easily grow through the branches of established hedges where they will provide added color and increased density to the hedge. Most of the procumbents have small flowers in a varied palette, some are perfumed, and several of them set hips after flowering.

'Bonica '82'

This is an exceptional variety that seems never to be without a flower for the whole of the summer and well into the autumn. From tiny buds emerge cupped, mid rose pink flowers that are tight and cupped, these gradually open to form almost flat, slightly frilled, more faded blooms with insignificant anthers of curious pinkish brown. They appear in clusters which invariably consist of flowers at many stages, from buds showing no sign of color to spent blooms. Foliage is healthy and dark and growth is bushy yet spreading.
Meilland, France, 1982, continuous flowering, 3 x 6 ft. (1 x 1.8 m)

Grouse is one of the most vigorous procumbents and will happily scramble over banks and through hedges.

'Fairyland'

I am fond of this little rose for, while it does not possess the vigorous qualities of some of its counterparts, it is very pretty and I personally find it to be highly scented. Flowers in bunches are fully double, cupped in shape, and soft pink fading to near white with age. Foliage is dark and glossy and, provided it is regularly deadheaded, it will flower for a long period. Growth is dense and capable of good, if not sudden coverage.
Harkness, UK, 1980, continuous flowering, 2 x 5 ft. (60 cm x 1.5 m)

'Grouse'

This can be a stunning rose in the right situation. While only producing scant repeat blooms, its first flush is magnificent and somewhat later than many garden roses, useful to remember when at the planning stage. Flowers are single and white from soft pink to white buds; leaves are dark and glossy, very much like *Rosa wichuraiana*, which is in its blood. Growth is vigorous and capable of many tasks. We have a couple of plants at our nursery, planted in a bed against a beech hedge. They have covered the bed and fought their way through and over the hedge. When in full flush they fill the adjacent parking lot with the most lovely perfume. Tiny hips follow in the autumn.
Kordes, Germany, 1982, repeat flowering, 2 x 10 ft. (60 cm x 3 m)

'Macrantha Raubritter'

Although to be correct this rose should be listed among the *Rosa macrantha* hybrids, I have not divided this directory so finely as to give them a separate section. However the habit of this rose warrants its inclusion here. Charming cupped semidouble flowers are mid- to soft rose pink in clusters. Branches are rather thorny and leaves generally gray-green. Can be a little prone to mildew but this is a once-flowering rose and attacks usually occur after flowering.
Kordes, Germany, 1967, summer flowering, 3 x 6 ft. (1 x 1.8 m)

'Summer Sunrise'

The result of a cross between 'Bonica '82' and 'New Dawn,' this rose displays qualities that can be attributed to both parents. Semidouble blooms are small and soft to bright pink. They open flat to display lovely golden stamens. Leaves are dark and glossy on vigorous growth. 'Summer Sunrise' is a free-flowering rose that, if deadheaded regularly, will produce blooms well into the autumn.
Beales, UK, 1994, continuous flowering, 18 in. x 3 ft.)(45 cm x 1 m)

Rugosas

Thorny, dense-growing plants with an upright habit, the rugosas are perfect intruder deterrents when planted along a boundary. Flowers appear regularly throughout the summer are, in many varieties, followed by splendid orange, tomato-shaped hips which are often of giant proportion. In accompaniment to the hips, the leaves will adopt various attractive hues in the autumn, from yellow through orange to umber, a combination that is stunningly beautiful. Rewarding even to the inexperienced gardener, in difficult conditions they make excellent sturdy hedges or are candidates for the mixed shrubbery.

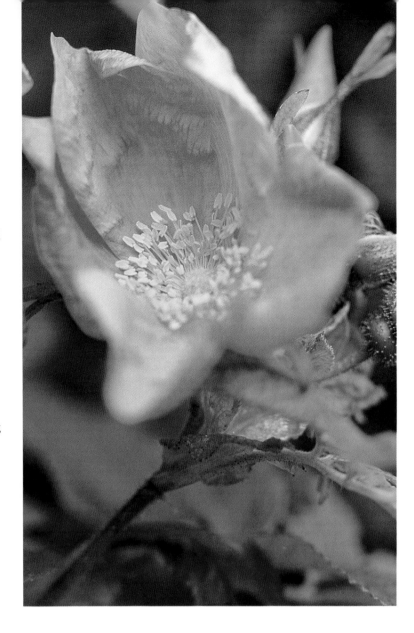

'Agnes'

This is hybrid of *Rosa rugosa* and *R. foetida persiana*, and owes its coloring to the latter of the two. Flowers are double, soft apricot-yellow, fading to near white with age and set off by dark leaves that are smaller than those of most Rugosas. Stems are well armed with nasty prickles. The odd flowers appear after the first flush which, in a good season, can be a truly lovely sight.
Saunders Central Experimental Farm, Canada, 1922, repeat flowering, 6 x 5 ft. (1.8 x 1.5 m)

'Belle Poitevine'

Due to crinkled petals, the flowers of this cultivar tend to have a rather unkempt appearance, that in many ways adds to their attractiveness. They are mid-silvery pink verging on lilac, scented, and have a golden coronet of anthers at the center. Leaves are bright green, heavily veined and healthy. A strong-growing plant that only occasionally sets hips.
Bruant, France 1894, repeat flowering 6 x 5 ft. (1.8 x 1.5 m)

'Blanc Double de Coubert'

Large flat flowers are pure white, double, and sweetly scented. This is an excellent, free-flowering rugosa, setting hips intermittently, with strong rich green foliage and many needle-like thorns. Lovely autumn leaves. A good candidate for hedging.
Cochet-Cochet, France, 1892, repeat flowering, 5 x 4 ft. (1.5 x 1.2 m)

'Roseraie de l'Hay'

A popular variety very often used in hedging. Blooms are large, semi-double, crimson-magenta, opening flat and ragged. They possess a strong clove-like scent. Flowers appear frequently throughout the summer and into autumn. Growth is bushy and thick, leaves bright rich green and heavily veined. Autumn coloring is stunning but it rarely sets hips.
Cochet-Cochet, France, 1901, continuous flowering, 6 x 5 ft. (1.8 x 1.5 m)

Rugosa roses are useful for hedging. Many of them will set impressive hips in the autumn.

'Scabrosa'

This rose is best known for the quality of its fruit, which are large, bright orange-red, and similar in shape to tomatoes. They often form early and are present on the plant at the same time as the flowers; these are large, single with almost wing like petals of rich silvery pink. Sweetly scented, they are borne amid heavily veined rich green leaves on an upright, dense growing plant. Has good autumn foliage.
Harkness, UK, 1960, continuous flowering, 6 x 4 ft. (1.8 x 1.2 m)

Species

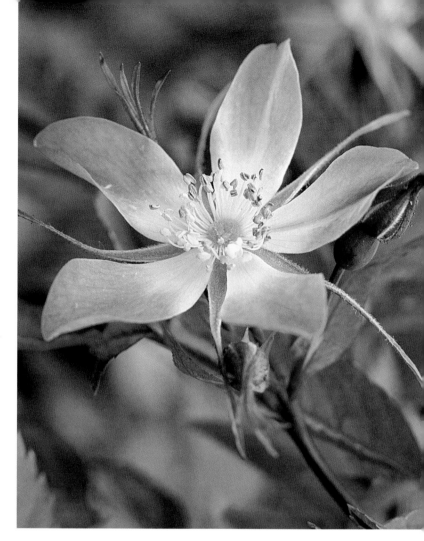

These are the predecessors to all modern-day hybrid roses; they are the wild or true roses of nature and, as such, although each one is significantly different to the others, they possess a natural, simple, and pure charm. The majority have single flowers, in varying shades but usually white or pink, followed by hips in different sizes, shapes, and in varying degrees of orange to red, and even mahogany and black in the case of *Rosa pimpinellifolia*. They are healthy roses when compared to hybrid varieties, and most are hardy. While having many similarities, the fact that they are unrelated to each other means that there are some very individual traits to be found in them. Some are early flowering, others produce blooms later on but very few are repeat flowering, they can be large or small in growth, with different shades and shapes of leaves. I value these roses greatly, for not only are they most important historically but they are delightful in themselves. It is interesting that while these roses are individually attributed as species, there is often more than one clone of each. This is because they have altered in some way, often only very slightly, by natural genetic modification in adapting to wider distribution in the wild, such as climate and soil in new locations. In the larger garden they can show off their characteristics, and are well suited to the conservation garden and useful additions to park and woodland.

Rosa canina

Also known as the 'Dog Rose.' This is the wild rose commonly found growing in hedges the length and breadth of Britain and in many American locations. Flowers are single, from blush pink to white, and are borne along lengths of arching branches, well dressed in narrow gray-green leaves, and heavily armed with thorns. Bright red hips follow in the autumn.
Europe, pre-1730, summer flowering, 6 x 10 ft. (1.8 x 3 m)

Rosa foetida

This is a charming, brightly colored rose. Single flowers are bright canary yellow with brown stamens. Young branches are tinged with plum and are endowed with long

Above: *Rosa glauca* has wonderful pewter gray foliage.

Below: *Rosa sericea pteracantha* has only four petals in each flower and stunning thorns.

spiteful thorns. Leaves are soft mid-gray-green and make up well populated leaflets. As the name suggests, the fragrance of this rose is not desirable. Closely related to it are *Rosa foetida bicolor*, which is bright orange-red, and *R. foetida persiana*, a double yellow that is largely responsible for the yellow coloring found in many modern roses and also sadly the cause of their proneness to blackspot. *Asia Minor, pre-1600, summer flowering, 8 x 5 ft. (2.5 x 1.5 m)*

Rosa glauca

Also known as *Rosa rubrifolia*. Possibly one of the best known species roses. Thornless stems are purple to red in color and are beautifully clothed with the main attraction of this rose, delightful pewter-gray leaves. The flowers are individually insignificant, even en masse they inspire little delight but in the autumn the hips that replace them do. Drooping bunches of

them are rather like cherries, and they are set off by lovely autumn coloring to the leaves.
Europe, 1830, summer flowering, 6 x 5 ft. (1.8 x 1.5 m)

Rosa sericea pteracantha

The appeal of this rose does not come from the flowers, but from the huge thorns that, without break, adorn the whole lengths of the arching branches. In shape they are wedge-like, tapering off to nasty hooked points. On young growth they are translucent with the sun behind them, a glowing shade of mahogany-red. The only significance of the flowers is the fact that they have only four petals, a feature found in this species only. Leaves are small and fern-like. There are one or two other closely related *sericea* species and only a few hybrids.
China, pre-1890, early summer flowering, 10 x 6 ft. (3 x 1.8 m)

Rosa virginiana

Reddish-brown stems produce only a few thorns. The leaves, which are bright green during the summer months, develop shades of amber and yellow changing to russet in the autumn, accompanied by polished red rotund hips. The flowers are beautiful, soft pink, sometimes dappled with a deeper shade. They are single and have beautiful prominent, dusty stamens.
North America, around 1807, summer flowering, 5 x 3 ft. (1.5 x 1 m)

'Lord Penzance' has apple scented leaves.

Sweetbriers or Eglanterias

These roses, with the odd exception, have deliciously apple-scented foliage that is strongest from young succulent shoots and leaves. It is best appreciated when the leaves are gently squeezed but it will pervade the air after rain, on damp dewy mornings and during balmy summers evenings. The collection we have available to us now is undoubtedly smaller than it was, for several have been lost over the years. Most of them will bear just one flush of flowers followed by hips in the autumn but there are one or two repeat-flowering sweetbriers, however, these are hybrids and tend not to have aromatic foliage. It is wise to cut back the sweetbriers to some extent to encourage the young growth that emits the most fragrance. These roses are perfect in natural settings, in wild or conservation areas but also are suited to the garden, where they are best in a mixed setting of other roses, shrubs, and perennials.

'Amy Robsart'

Blooms are semisingle, bright but deep glowing pink with white at their centers where they have a coronet of yellow stamens. When in full flush this rose is spectacular. Leaves are not overly perfumed, but they are tough and clothe vigorous arching, slightly angular branches. A hardy variety tolerant of shade and poor soil.
Penzance, UK, 1890s, summer flowering, 10 x 8 ft. (3 x 2.5 m)

'Lady Penzance'

The foliage of this lovely rose is among the most highly scented in this little group and is tough and leathery. Pretty flowers are single, copper to salmon with hints of pink changing to yellow at their centers with bold yellow stamens. Bright red hips follow the flowers in the autumn. A strong-growing variety, tolerant of most situations.
Penzance, UK, 1890s, summer flowering, 7 x 6 ft. (2.1 x 1.8 m)

'Lord Penzance'

This gentleman was responsible for several sweetbriers in the latter years of the 19th century. Flowers are soft buff-yellow with a suggestion of pink and has pronounced golden stamens. This variety hips well in the autumn and, along with 'Lady Penzance,' has nicely scented foliage.
Penzance, UK, 1890s, summer flowering 7 x 6 ft. (2.1 x 1.8 m)

'Meg Merrilies'

An excellent variety with crimson red, semidouble blooms in profusion in midsummer, the coloring of the petals is a contrast to the bright yellow stamens found within them. Both flowers and leaves are scented. A strong growing, tough variety that is well armed with thorns. Hips well later in the year.
Penzance, UK, 1890s, summer flowering, 8 x 7 ft. (2.5 x 2.1 m)

Teas

These are not the hardiest of roses, but there are some delightfully beautiful, heavily perfumed varieties. In colder climates it is a good idea to grow them in pots so that they can be overwintered in a cool greenhouse or conservatory otherwise they will require some protection in winter. It is difficult to fault them with anything other than their tenderness, except that some of them produce blooms of such size that they cause the fragile branches to bow under their weight. They originated in the Far East where Sir Abraham Hume discovered *Rosa indica odorata*, now more frequently known as 'Hume's Blush,' in 1810. It is thought that this rose, along with a few other teas, was transported to Europe aboard ships belonging to the East India Tea Company, hence their name, but others suggest that the name they hold is a comparison to their perfume. Not according to my nose.

'Archiduc Joseph' has many colors in its intricate flowers.

'Archiduc Joseph'

The muddled, flat flowers of this wonderful rose are made up from a palette including pink, copper, apricot, and purple with hints of yellow here and there; this combination may sound awful, but the effect is most lovely. One of the hardier teas with purple-tinted young growth and leaves and very few thorns. Placed against a wall it can be grown as a small climber.
G. Nabonnand,
France, 1872,
continuous flowering,
5 x 3 ft. (1.5 x 1 m)

'Clementina Carbonieri'

The coloring of the flowers on this delightful rose is similar in all respects to 'Archiduc Joseph' except that they are more muted. They are scented and a little shaggy, almost quartered in style. Foliage is dark and glossy on a bushy plant and is ideal in a pot, placed in a good location in the garden.
Bonfiglioli, Italy, 1913,
continuous flowering,
3 x 2 ft. (1 m x 60 cm)

'Lady Hillingdon'

The apricot blooms of this superb rose start out from a long pointed bud opening shaggy and loose and they exude a fantastic perfume. Young leaves and shoots are deep plum-purple, a contrasting foil for the blooms. Growth is not hardy but this rose will get through most winters even if damaged by the frost. A climbing form is also available.
Lowe and Shawyer,
UK, 1910,
continuous flowering
3 x 2 ft. (1 m x 60 cm)

'Mme. Bravy'

An old tea rose and a very beautiful one. Double flowers are large and blowsy, creamy white tinged blush with a strong perfume, which is said by some to be reminiscent of tea and by others, of raspberries. They appear in abundance on a dense, well foliated bush that is ideal in size for growing in a container.
Guillot Père, France, 1846,
continuous flowering
3 x 2 ft. (1 m x 60 cm)

'Tipsy Imperial Concubine'

Discovered in China by Mrs. Hazel le Rougetel, this is thought to be an old Chinese cultivar. Large globular flowers are soft pink, overlaid with shades of yellow and sometimes tinged red. It is scented and very free flowering. Growth bushy.
Beales, UK, 1982,
continuous flowering,
2 x 2 ft. (60 x 60 cm)

Climbing and Rambling Roses

The differences between climbing and rambling roses

When it comes to roses, one of the most frequently asked questions is what is the difference between a climber and a rambler? To simplify the answer one could say that climbers climb and ramblers ramble, which is a useful rule of thumb when selecting varieties and probably the most relevant factor when deciding on which is right for a specific purpose. It is also generally true that ramblers are more vigorous, but there are more precise differences than these. Climbers flower on growth produced earlier in the same season but ramblers only flower on the growth they made in the previous season, which is why pruning methods are different for each group. Many climbers flower repeatedly or continuously throughout the summer months, while ramblers usually have just one flush, often followed by hips in the autumn. Generally ramblers being more vigorous, will cope with demanding duties such as growing through the branches of trees or over unsightly buildings, for example, while climbers are happier when growing on pillars, against trellis or walls. With both climbers and ramblers, it will probably take two or three years before they begin to look established and often this long before the very vigorous ramblers start to flower. It is also interesting to note that some of the most vigorous procumbent (ground cover) roses perform well as ramblers and, conversely, if left to tumble, many ramblers will cover the ground.

CLIMBERS

Climbing Bourbons

This is a small group, but within its ranks are some of the loveliest climbing roses. It is true that some of the shrub Bourbons can be grown as small climbers with support but the ones I include here are much more vigorous than them. Most flower abundantly, a few over a long season, but their best attraction must be the perfume they exude. If a fault can be found at all with these roses it is their tendency to mildew later in the season. To avoid this or at least keep its attack to a minimum try to plant them in open, airy positions and avoid very dry spots.

'Blairii No.2'

This is a truly magnificent variety when in full flower and, although any later blooming will not obliterate the foliage in the way that the first does, the flowers are still delightful. The large blooms are double pale pink deepening toward the center, and they are very fragrant. Foliage is mid-green and shiny.
Blair, UK, 1845,
repeat flowering,
12 x 6 ft. (3.8 x 1.8 m)

'Souvenir de la Malmaison, Climbing'

As with it's bushy counterpart, this variety has the most beautiful flat and quartered blooms of soft powder pink to ivory. They are exquisitely perfumed but do hate wet weather when they easily become balled, the remedy for this is to tease open the outer damaged petals, allowing those within to develop properly; this must be done in haste though, before the base of all the petals decays.
Bennett, UK, 1893,
repeat flowering
12 x 8 ft. (3.8 x 2.5 m)

'Zéphirine Drouhin'

This rose has much sentimental value for me, for a bloom of it was laid on the font for my christening, my father had flowers of it imported for my wedding and, in turn, I had a bloom of it present at the christening of my daughter. It has two or three splendid qualities: it is thornless, highly perfumed, and capable of flowering well into the autumn. Flowers are deep cerise pink, semidouble and a little muddled.
Bizot, France, 1868,
continuous flowering,
10 x 6 ft. (3 x 1.8 m)

'Blairii No. 2' is one of the most beautiful of the climbing Bourbons.

Boursaults

This is a group like no other, and there is no positive evidence to suggest from which roses they originally descended. While they mostly flower only once on growth from the previous season, I include them here with other climbers, as their growth habit cannot in any way be described as rambling. They are all thornless and share the attributes of arching smooth stems and long pointed foliage. Blooms, too, bear similarities to each other, being generally rather unkempt and in the more double forms almost quartered. In coloring they are all similar also ranging from mid-pink to pinkish red.

'Amadis'

Also known as 'Crimson Boursault.' The semidouble medium-sized flowers of crimson-purple are slightly cupped and a little unkempt when fully open. They can be found borne singly or in small clusters. Mature wood is plum colored. At its happiest it may produce the odd repeat bloom but it is generally summer flowering only.
France, 1829,
summer flowering,
10 x 6 ft. (3 x 1.8 m)

'Blush Boursault'

Beautiful flowers are pale, blush pink, and double. Growth is less purple than some, but still heavily colored and leaves are a dark, matt green. This is more vigorous member of the Boursault group.
France, 1848,
summer flowering,
15 x 10 ft. (4.5 x 3m)

'Mme. Sancy de Parabère'

Mid- to soft pink petals are laid out in an almost quartered style, with those outermost usually slightly softer than those in the center. Leaves are dark and characteristically thin and pointed and wood is more brown than purple on mature plants.
France, mid-1870s,
summer Flowering
15 x 10 ft. (4.5 x 3 m)

'Morlettii'

Double flowers are magenta to pink with petals furling inward quite tightly at the center of the flower but more loosely displayed around at the edges. As it is less vigorous than the other Boursaults, it can make a useful, free standing shrub rose, especially with the benefit of some support.
France, 1880s,
summer flowering,
8 x 6 ft. (2.5 x 1.8 m)

Above: 'Mme Grégoire Staechelin' is one of the first roses to bloom each year.'

Below: 'Mme. Sancy de Parabère' has typical ragged flowers.

Climbing hybrid teas

The climbing hybrid teas are the result of a bush hybrid tea, suddenly and without any apparent reason, sending out a long, arching, climbing branch. As with all things unexpected, the perpetuation of the climbing capabilities of these roses came about only by chance: a knowledgeable gardener or nurseryman must have realized that what was before him was more than a gangly branch and had material from it taken for propagation rather than simply pruning it back, as many gardeners would do. Thanks to their wits we now have a race of excellent climbing roses. While their bush counterparts flower more or less continuously, the climbers found here have a mad flush with a repeat blooming in late summer to early autumn. They excel as climbers but will need training and pruning to prevent them from becoming naturally top heavy.

'Château de Clos Vougeot'

The blooms are double and deep red, handing out an expensive perfume, the texture of the petals can only be compared to velvet. As with many climbing hybrid teas, the dark foliage is fairly spaced out, revealing strong, relatively thornless stems. A vigorous if somewhat angular growing variety.
Morse, UK, 1920,
summer flowering,
15 x 8 ft. (5.4 x 2.5 m)

'Cupid'

Blooms are large, single, soft flesh to powder pink, nearing primrose at the center with delightful golden anthers. A mature plant will produce many blooms at once but very few if any later on. Growth can be angular and a little cumbersome with sparse foliage but this is not a problem if it can be grown intermingled with a better-clothed plant. Large plump hips, of pale orange, follow the flowers. A good rose well worth space in the garden.
B.R. Cant, UK, 1915,
summer flowering,
10 x 6 ft. (3 x 1.8 m)

'Étoile de Hollande, Climbing'

Perhaps the biggest fault of the bush form of this rose is that it hangs its head, preventing the onlooker from fully partaking in its glory. This is perhaps the best point about the climbing form: those looking at the blooms can enjoy their perfection as they nod down toward them. Fully double, these nodding flowers are deep velvety red and share with those partaking a wonderful perfume. With age the red turns to purple, especially in full sun. Leaves are deep green and young growth tinged beetroot.
Leenders, Holland, 1931,
summer flowering,
12 x 8 ft. (3.8 x 2.5 m)

'Mme. Grégoire Staechelin'

One of the most inspiring garden roses as it is one of the first double-flowered, highly scented varieties to bloom each year, giving a promise of all those to follow. Loosely double, large almost bell-like flowers are soft pink, a little deeper on the outside and appear in profusion in late spring to early summer, with the odd repeating bloom later on. Foliage is a little coarse but growth is reasonably vigorous. Huge hips appear later on if the plant is not deadheaded.
Dot, Spain, 1927,
repeat flowering,
15 x 10 ft. (4.5 x 3 m)

'Mme. Caroline Testout, Climbing'

The flowers of this rose are like miniature cabbages, although rose pink as opposed to green. They really are fully double to the extent that they are globular with the tips of the outer petals reflexing until they are fully open. The perfume they emit is wonderful. As with most in this group, the leaves are well spaced, and growth can be angular, but this is easily overcome with training. A good rose that will produce the odd second bloom.
Ketten Bros,
Luxembourg, 1921,
repeat flowering,
12 x 8 ft. (3.8 x 2.5 m)

Climbing Floribundas

As with the climbing hybrid teas, climbing floribundas are the result of the bush version of the variety having produced a sport, in other words developing a shoot with climbing capabilities. Propagation material taken from this branch resulted in plants with total climbing capabilities. The flowers of the climbing form are in all respects identical to the bush form but they usually only appear in one abundant flush, while their shorter-growing kin will flower pretty well nonstop during the summer and into the autumn. There are not many commercially available, but those that are can be useful additions to the garden.

'Allgold, Climbing'

Well known for its strong yellow, unfading blooms, 'Allgold' is a useful climber when a bright color is needed. They are semidouble, of average size, lightly perfumed, and are offset by dark and glossy foliage.. The clusters, or occasional single flowers are held erect on strong stems. A good all-round climber.
Gandy, UK, 1961,
summer flowering,
15 x 10 ft. (4.5 x 3 m)

The climbing version of 'Allgold' is a sport of the bush form.

'Iceberg, Climbing'

Iceberg is a famous rose, and the climbing form deserves similar recognition. Flowers emerge from cream buds, opening pure white and semidouble in small clusters. Sadly not fragrant but certainly abundant. Leaves are no more than mid-green, sometimes pale green, but the contrast with the white may make them seem darker. A climber of reasonable vigor with flexible growth that is easily trained.
Cants, UK, 1968, summer flowering, 18 x 10 ft. (5 x 3 m)

'Masquerade, Climbing'

Perhaps not my favorite variety but useful when bright shocking color is needed. Semidouble blooms open yellow and change as they mature through shades of orange and pink to red, they are borne in clusters. Stems are thorny and vigorous and clothed in dark, fairly healthy foliage.
Gregory, UK, 1958, summer flowering, 18 x 10 ft. (5 x 3 m)

'Queen Elizabeth, Climbing'

The bush form of 'Queen Elizabeth' is one of the most vigorous floribundas, so it stands to reason that the climbing form is capable of reaching great heights. Blooms are large, silvery pink in clusters, and are moderately fragrant. Leaves too are large and leathery. This variety needs careful pruning and training to prevent it from becoming top heavy.
Wheatcroft, UK, 1960, summer flowering, 20 x 10 ft. (6 x 3 m)

Modern Climbers

In common with the modern shrub roses, these climbers have such diverse parentage that they do not fall into any other specific classification, therefore in order to give them a title they are grouped together under this heading. Among their ranks are some excellent roses of varying characteristics, from hugely vigorous to shorter-growing varieties. There is a modern climber available in any natural rose color, some are highly perfumed, some not much. I probably need not go on. This is a large group of roses, and it is impossible to include them all here, so I have selected a range with various colors and styles.

'Aloha'

Not the most vigorous climber, in fact probably better described as a pillar rose. The blooms are very double, deep rose pink with the occasional hint of salmon and magenta; they are superbly perfumed. Foliage is dark and glossy on an upright plant that is seldom without flower.
Boerner, USA, 1949, continuous flowering, 10 x 6 ft. (3 x 1.8 m)

Aloha is best used as a pillar rose.

'City of York'

I grow to love this rose more each time I see it. The semidouble flowers open cupped from creamy yellow buds, then become creamy white with hints of lemon at the center where they display a crown of golden stamens. They are lightly perfumed and are produced freely and abundantly, often giving a second flush in autumn. Foliage is dark and glossy and growth pliable; an easy rose to train.
Tantau, Germany, 1960, summer flowering, 15 x 10 ft. (4.5 x 3 m)

'Dublin Bay'

Double flowers of average proportions are deep, unfading, blood red, cupped in shape and quite beautiful. They are borne in small clusters continuously throughout the summer and well into the autumn. Foliage is healthy mid-green and very glossy. Its upright habit allows it to be grown as a large shrub, otherwise it is best on a pillar.
McGredy, UK, 1976, continuous flowering, 7 x 5 ft. (2.1 x 1.5 m)

'Eden Rose '88'

A shorter-growing climber very much in the old-fashioned style. The large flowers are very double, almost a perfect ball until they are fully open, creamy white to blush blending with deeper pink edging to the petals. They are borne in small clusters against dark foliage. Not that vigorous in growth, but free flowering over a long season.
Meilland, France, 1987, continuous flowering, 8 x 6 ft. (2.5 x 1.8 m)

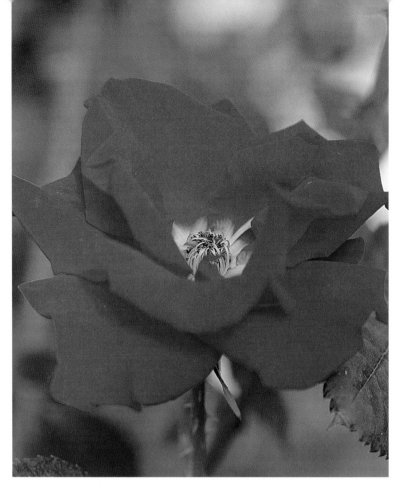

Noisettes

The noisettes are among the most beautiful climbing roses in my opinion. They are refined roses, in soft shades of pink and white and particularly yellow not at all garish, just perfectly natural. There are vigorous varieties and those less so, one or two very hardy ones, and a few that may need careful siting to protect them from the worst of winter weather. They are relatively easy to grow in the garden and, although some may have a susceptibility to mildew later in the season, they are generally healthy.

'Golden Showers'

This is another well-known climber of average proportions. Large blooms are semidouble, shaggy, deep golden yellow at first fading as they mature to a creamy yellow shade and display dark contrasting anthers. Leaves are dark and glossy, a superb foil to the flowers and growth is upright and a little bushy. Flowers well into the autumn.
Lammerts, USA, 1956,
continuous flowering,
10 x 6 ft. (3 x 1.8 m)

'Leverkusen'

A superb and healthy yellow climber. Lemon yellow flowers are double, rosette like in shape, sweetly scented with crinkled petals. They appear continuously, with the odd break throughout the

summer, against dark, leathery deeply veined foliage. Growth is vigorous, slender and easy to tie in. This climber will grow well in almost any aspect and will cope with poor soils.
Kordes, Germany, 1954,
continuous flowering,
10 x 8 ft. (3 x 2.5 m)

'Swan Lake'

The flowers of this variety are at their most beautiful when the petals first begin to unfurl. They are white with flesh pink tones and deeper pink shades at the base maturing to near pure white and are freely produced in small clusters. Foliage is dark and growth upright and tidy. A good pillar rose.
McGredy, UK, 1968,
continuous flowering,
8 x 6 ft. (2.5 x 1.8 m)

Above: 'Parkdirektor Riggers' has glossy leaves.

Below: 'Mme Alfred Carrière' copes in poor situations.

'Alister Stella Gray'

Borne in clusters, the slightly muddled flowers which consist of small, almost folded petals are soft yellow with deeper centers. They are flat and scented. Foliage is dark and growth slender and relatively thornless. The first flush of flowers is always the best but you do occasionally get further odd blooms later on.
A H Gray, UK 1894,
repeat flowering,
15 x 10 ft. (4.5 x 3 m)

'Blush Noisette'

An excellent little rose of accommodating proportions that can be grown as a large shrub if given support. Not vigorous, so patience will be needed when wanting it to climb. From deep pink, tubby buds emerge small flowers in large clusters. They are soft pink, with tints of lilac, fading with age. Leaves are dark green on dark wood that carries few thorns.
Noisette, USA, 1825,
continuous flowering ,
7 x 4 ft. (2.1 x 1.2 m)

'Céline Forestier'

The blooms of this variety are larger than those of 'Alister Stella Gray' with more petals, and are a more intense yellow with a faint tinge of pink. They open flat with in-furled center petals. A free-flowering variety that flowers late into the season. Growth is pliable and foliage a light green. A smaller climber that is happy grown in the confines of a pot.
Trouillard, France, 1842,
continuous flowering,
8 x 4 ft. (2.5 x 1.2 m)

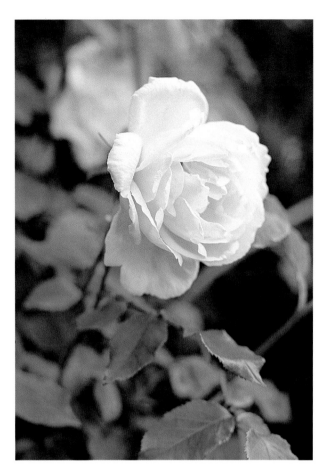

Climbing Teas

The climbing tea roses need careful placing in positions that will protect them against the worst of the winter weather, as they are not very hardy. If this is possible they will repay you with beautiful flowers and fantastic perfume. This is not a large group of roses and sadly many have been lost over the years, probably because of their tenderness.

'Adam'

The beautiful, heavily scented blooms of this rose are large, double and best described as buff to apricot with an overlay of pink. When open they are almost quartered. Ample leaves are dark and large and growth is not vigorous. an be grown as a large shrub in the right situation and is happy in a pot.
Adam, UK, 1833,
repeat flowering ,
7 x 5 ft. (2.1 x 1.5 m)

'Gloire de Dijon'

A favorite climber with large, quartered flowers of buff apricot with tinges of salmon toward the base of the petals. It has a very strong, heady perfume. Growth is vigorous with young shoots tinged with bronze. Other leaves are dark green and plentiful. Although this is one of the most beautiful roses, it hates wet weather, when the flowers become balled as the outer petals stick together. The only remedy for this is to carefully tease them away so that the remaining petals may unfurl.
Jacotot, France, 1853,
repeat flowering,
12 x 8 ft. (3.8 x 2.5 m)

'Sombreuil'

This is one of my favorites. Large white rosette-shaped flowers open flat from fat buds of cream. They are chiefly white with pinky apricot at the base of the petals. The perfume they emit is outstanding. Growth is vigorous and easily trained, leaves dark, and on the whole healthy. Flowers freely with often a second flush.
Robert, France, 1843,
repeat flowering,
10 x 8 ft. (3 x 2.5 m)

'Souvenir de Mme. Léonie Viennot, Climbing'

This is a lovely rose which was reintroduced in England by my father. He had been given budwood from a friend whose mother had sent it, wrapped in polyethylene in a pencil case, from New Zealand. Individual flowers are not huge, soft yellow heavily tinged with salmon, the overall effect is charming. They are fragrant on a fairly vigorous plant with dark green leaves.
Bernaix, France, 1897,
repeat flowering,
12 x 8 ft. (3.8 x 2.5 m)

Left: 'Céline Forrestier' is a beautiful, scented climbing rose.

Opposite: 'Sombreuil' is a versatile, very free-flowering, and heavily scented climber.

'Desprez à Fleurs Jaune'

Flowers are smaller than many in this group, cascading in clusters they are a delicate buff to pink shade, opening loose and blowsy. They exude a fresh fruity perfume. This is a vigorous noisette which is easily trained. It is tolerant of shade and poor soil and makes a good tree climber.
Desprez, France, 1835,
repeat flowering,
20 x 10 ft. (6 x 3 m)

'Mme. Alfred Carrière'

Given that this rose is over a century old it is still very popular today, not only because it will grow well on a cool wall and in shade, but because it is exquisitely beautiful. Shaggy, double blooms are creamy white with the odd tinge of pink and are heavily perfumed. Leaves are light to mid-green and growth is slender and relatively thorn free.
J. Schwartz, France, 1879,
continuous flowering,
15 x 10 ft. (4.5 x 3 m)

Ramblers

The Arvensis Hybrids

Having derived from Britain's native "field rose," this group (also known as ayreshires) pairs its hardiness with naturally dignified simplicity. They serve many purposes; for growth their habits make them well suited to scrambling across the ground, intermingling with other ramblers, and to reaching some quite considerable heights in the garden. On the whole they are quite thorny and share a tendency to dark plum-colored new growth.

'Venusta Pendula'
An ancient variety which was reintroduced to the market in the early 1900s. Pink buds open to reveal double white, flushed pink clusters of unscented small flowers. Growth can be twiggy but young shoots are deep plum maroon and the foliage is a dark, foil for the blooms. A reasonably vigorous variety. *Kordes, Germany, 1928, summer flowering, 18 x 10 ft. (5 x 3 m)*

Right: Rosa arvensis is a native of Europe commonly called the "field rose."

Below: 'Dundee Rambler' is very hardy.

'Janet B. Wood'
This variety was rediscovered by a Mrs. McQueen of Ayrshire, Scotland and reintroduced by my father. Small flowers are double, white, and held in clusters on a strong-growing plant with dark plentiful foliage and wood that is also dark in color. It is believed to be the original double Ayrshire rose first introduced in 1768. It will cope with all situations from poor soil and shade to a cool, dark aspect and is relatively vigorous. *Originally introduced in 1768, re-introduced by Beales, UK, 1984, summer flowering , 15 x 10 ft. (4.5 x 3 m)*

'Dundee Rambler'
This charming rose was bred in Scotland around the year 1850. I find the double, in-furled white-tinged pink blooms quite delightful; they are borne in large nodding clusters set off by splendid dark leaves. Growth is dense, vigorous, and thorny on a hardy plant with the capability of covering many an eyesore, such as a tumbledown shed or dead tree. *Martin, Scotland, around 1850, summer flowering, 20 x 10 ft. (6 x 3 m)*

Moschata Ramblers

Also referred to as the musk ramblers, this small group includes some beautiful roses. Those I describe below are closely related to *Rosa moschata,* but there are many more varieties with moschata blood somewhere in their history.

'Paul's Himalayan Musk'

This must be one of the best known, small-flowered pink ramblers, and it should be. It was first introduced by William Paul in 1882, a breeder and authority of the time responsible for a number of roses that are still very popular today. Its small pompon-like flowers of soft powdery pink are produced in large bunches amid large drooping leaves. It is very vigorous and will send out long growths like fishing rods, on which it produces flowers the following season.
Paul, UK, late 19th century,
summer flowering,
20 x 12 ft. (6 x 3.8 m)

'Narrow Water'

A less vigorous rose and worth inclusion as it is an excellent all-round grower with lovely flowers and a capability of producing more than one flush in each season, often well into the autumn. The blooms are semi double, soft pink in clusters, and are scented. Dark leaves provide a perfect background to them. Can be grown as a shrub.
Daisy Hill Nurseries,
Ireland, about 1883,
repeat flowering,
8 x 6 ft. (2.5 x 1.8 m)

'Princess of Nassau'

A little known variety but a favorite of mine in that its flower coloring, being chiefly white is tinged with an ochre yellow. Semidouble and sporting a coronet of dusty orange anthers, the flowers are most attractive. This variety flowers in the summer and then again in the autumn, a useful quality. It was rediscovered by the eminent rosarian Graham Thomas who supplied my father with budwood to enable its reintroduction in 1982, although it is considerably older than this.
Of unknown origin but probably early 19th century
Repeat flowering
10 x 8 ft. (3 x 2.5 m)

'The Garland'

I include this one not only because it is an excellent rose but also because of sentimental reasons. I spent a large part of my childhood living in an old farm house, where a specimen of 'The Garland' grew close to my bedroom window and each year I would enjoy its delicious perfume as it wafted into my bedroom. I am taken back to this room every time I smell this rose. Flowers are semidouble, white tinged pink, and appear in great profusion in midsummer. Leaves are mid-to dark green and there is an ample covering of vicious hooked thorns.
Wills, UK, 1835,
summer flowering,
15 x 10 ft. (4.5 x 3 m)

Multiflora Ramblers

The direct descendants of *Rosa multiflora* are the most easy to identify but there are very many more fused with other groups and less obvious when it comes to lineage. Among the ranks of these ramblers are some of the best known and indeed most stunning ramblers available, many of them with the vigor to navigate their way through the branches of tall trees, over garden buildings, large pergolas, to the top and indeed along large expanses of wall.

'Bobbie James'

This is a beautiful rambler with semisingle, slightly cupped, pure white flowers borne in clusters against large fresh green leaves. It was introduced in 1961 and compared to many others of its nature, has come to equal and in some cases surpass them.

It is strong in growth with well-armed branches and is capable of naturally scrambling through a hedge. It is tolerant of poor soils and shade and will cope on a cool shady wall.
Sunningdale Nurseries,
UK, 1961,
summer flowering,
30 x 20 ft. (9 x 6 m)

'Bobbie James' can reach a height of thirty feet.

'Francis E. Lester'

Another beautiful multi-flora with individual flowers that are more dainty and, dare I say, more feminine than those of 'Bobbie James.' They are single, slightly cupped, white with pink around the edges of petals, and are perfumed. Small rounded hips follow in autumn. Leaves are dark, slim and elegant. It is a very popular garden rose.
Lester Rose Gardens,
USA, 1946,
summer flowering,
15 x 10 ft. (4.5 x 3 m)

'Ghislaine de Féligonde'

One of the few ramblers that break the once-flowering pattern, this variety will produce a good second flush and will still be flowering in early autumn. It is most attractive and a little different in growth habit to the majority of the multifloras; it is certainly less vigorous than many and produces dense rather than tall coverage. Flowers, in clusters are fully double, open in a shade of apricot orange, sometimes tinged pink and pale with age to a soft shade of buff.
Turbat, France, 1916,
repeat flowering,
8 x 8 ft. (2.5 x 2.5 m)

Left:
'Rambling Rector' also often called **'Shakespeare's Musk'** is ideal climbing through the branches of trees.

Opposite: **'Ghislaine de Féligonde'** is a smaller rambler, that produces flowers for most of the summer.

Sempervirens Hybrids

In the Victorian era, these roses were referred to as the evergreen roses and this is true for, in all but severe winters, they do retain their foliage. They are a dense-growing and, on the whole, vigorous group with pompon-style flowers.

'Adélaide d'Orléans'

Soft pink and gently fragrant small blooms are borne in clusters en masse in midsummer. Foliage is dense on a plant with reasonable vigor. This French rose will tolerate poor soils and shade, useful through tree branches or where dense cover is needed.
Jacques, France, 1826, summer flowering, 15 x 10 ft. (4.5 x 3 m)

'Félicité Perpétue'

From clusters of small but plump buds emerge tight pompon flowers of creamy white with pink edging that are softly scented. Leaves are glossy and dark and will remain on the plant until the nastiest of frosts forces them to fall; stems are not overly endowed with thorns. A good, vigorous if not overwhelming rambler of beauty. There is a dwarf form of this rose, 'White Pet' that rarely exceeds a metre in height but will bloom well into the autumn.
Jacques, France, 1827, summer flowering, 15 x 10 ft. (4.5 x 3 m)

'Spectabilis'

Creamy white flowers are tinged with lilac and nod in large clusters from an unassuming plant with dark green, semievergreen foliage. This is an old and reliable variety, tolerant of all but the most severe conditions; it is a good all-rounder which may occasionally produce a bloom or two after its first flush.
Of unknown origin, about 1850, summer flowering, 10 x 6 ft. (3 x 1.8 m)

'Rambling Rector'

This is a very old and well known cultivar, sometimes known as 'Shakespeare's Musk.' Flowers are small, semidouble creamy white, fading to pure white with age, and appear in large clusters, pervading the air with their fragrance. Growth is extremely vigorous, and I am fond of seeing this variety growing through the branches of tree where the nodding clusters of flowers are well displayed against the greenery of the leaves. Clusters of hips replace the flowers later in the year.
Of unknown origin, but very old, summer flowering, 20 x 15 ft. (6.x 4.5 m)

'Veilchenblau'

There are a few ramblers available in shades of lilac and purple and this is one of them. Semidouble flowers are violet-purple, flecked white fading to a gray shade of lilac with maturity. It is vigorous and strong growing and a good companion to the softer-shaded varieties.
Schmidt, Germany, 1909, summer flowering, 6.x 4.5m (20 x 15ft)

Other Classified Ramblers

The three varieties included here do not belong to any of the larger groups that appear in this section but to other, smaller classifications that I have not included. However, I did not wish to leave these three varieties out as they are important roses. Their classification is noted after the name.

'Kiftsgate' (*filipes*)

One of the best known "tree climbers" with magnificent climbing capability. The single, scented cream to white flowers are borne in huge trusses, and are followed by many small hips in the autumn. Growth is extremely vigorous with large bright green foliage and copper tinted young shoots. It will tolerate cool, dark aspects, shade and poor soil.
Murrell, UK, 1954,
summer flowering,
30 x 20 ft. (9 x 6 m)

'Mermaid' (*bracteata*)

The wonderful flowers of this rose are large, with wing-like petals, bright lemon yellow with pronounced stamens and a gentle fragrance. The almost evergreen foliage is large, rich green and glossy on slender growth that is well armed with nasty hooked thorns. It tolerates shade, but does not like frost and will die back in bad winters.
W. Paul, UK, 1917,
continuous flowering,
30 x 20 ft. (9 x 6 m)

Right:
'Sir Cedric Morris' has large, soft gray leaves and is very vigorous.

Below:
'Kiftsgate' is extremely fast growing.

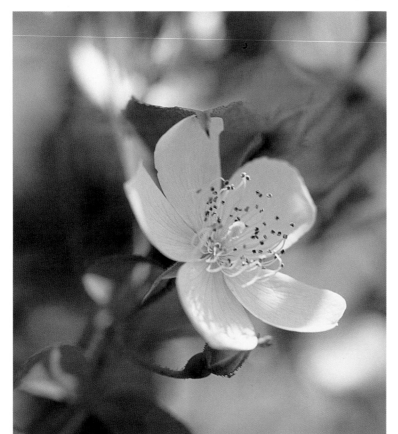

'Sir Cedric Morris' (*glauca*)

This was one of a number of *Rosa glauca* seedlings found growing in the garden of the late Sir Frederick Ashton, and it is a staggering sight. Blooms are small and single in huge trusses with small orange-red hips following later, but it is the foliage I love best. It is soft gray, large, and drooping in habit, a beautiful background to the flowers but also a feature in its own right. This is a very vigorous rose, ideal for growing through the branches of trees, and will cope with the usual dryness at the roots there.
Beales, UK, 1979,
summer flowering,
30 x 20 ft. (9 x 6 m)

Species Ramblers

While the majority of species roses are the forerunners of one or another race, or indeed several races of roses, they are also distinct in that they are the pure roses of nature. They are the only roses to grow true to type from seed, although there are some with slightly differing clones. They are an important group of roses that we should very much respect. Although some consider species roses to be boring, these people should look at them a little harder. Most are exquisite in their simple beauty and most, in fact nearly all, are far less prone to the effects of disease than hybrid roses.

Rosa arvensis

Also known as "field rose," *Rosa arvensis* is a native of Britain (in fact Britain's only native with climbing capabilities) and can be found creeping through wild hedges, especially in southern England, hence its other name. It is strikingly beautiful with pure white single flowers bearing a ring of bright golden anthers set off by dark foliage and dark pliable stems. It is worth growing as a garden rose if you have the space and will give a lovely display of hips in the autumn.
Europe,
summer flowering,
20 x 10 ft. (6 x 3 m)

Rosa helenae

I choose to include *Rosa helenae* as, in my opinion, it is one of the most beautiful, dainty-flowered, species ramblers. It was originally was found growing wild in China by E. H. Wilson who named it after his wife. A vigorous rose, it produces large corymbs of single white blooms that are followed by glorious, small red hips in the autumn.
Wilson, China, 1907,
summer flowering,
20 x 15 ft. (6.x 4.5 m)

Rosa moschata

This is a very ancient rose, although there is no positive evidence of its original homeland, possibly Southern China or India. It is important in the family tree of roses for it has many descendants, both direct and indirect. Unlike *Rosa helenae* it does not reach huge proportions and is a little later flowering than many, usually producing its blooms in mid- to late summer. Flowers are creamy white, single in form and flat, held in large clusters. Probably due to its later flowering period it does not always set hips.
16th century,
summer flowering,
8 x 6 ft. (2.5 x 1.8 m)

Rosa mulliganii

I include this in my limited choice of species rambling roses not because it is hugely important in history to the rose, but because it deserves space in the garden today. Small white flowers are single, held in clusters and exude a wonderful delicate fragrance with a banana-like aroma. Leaves are gray-green, tinted purple when young. A fairly vigorous rose, which was often, until recently, misnamed *Rosa longicuspis.*
China, 1917,
summer flowering,
15 x 10 ft. (4.5 x 3 m)

Rosa multiflora

This variety was, until recently, often used as an understock and is a strong-growing hardy species. As with *Rosa moschata* it has

Rosa arvensis is extremely hardy.

many important descendants, most of which are also hardy and strong growing. When mature it will produce small, creamy white blooms in huge abundance followed by orange-red oval fruits. This is a rose tolerant of most poor growing situations.
Asia, 12th century,
summer flowering,
15 x 10 ft. (4.5 x 3 m)

Rosa wichuraiana

Discovered in China in 1860 by the German plant collector, Max Ernst Wichura, this is an interesting rose that is responsible for many offspring. Flowers in clusters are neat and white followed by small orange vermilion hips in the autumn. One particular trait, well demonstrated in many of the hybrid Wichuraianas, is its extremely glossy dark foliage. I include it in this section as it is difficult to include elsewhere given the breakdown I have elected to use. It could also be listed as a procumbent or climbing rose (it is as well suited to sprawling over banks and through hedges), and many of its direct offspring are regularly listed in both categories. This is a useful rambling rose.
Wilson, 1860,
summer flowering,
6 x 20 ft. (1.8 x 6 m)

Wichuraiana Hybrids

While *Rosa wichuraiana* is, in essence, a rambler with diverse uses (good on a wall, scrambling through hedges and over banks or into trees). Its offspring could easily be split in two groups, some falling into the rambling category and fewer others with more of a climbing tendency. This is due largely to interbreeding, some resulting hybrids tending to scramble and produce just one flush of flowers each year, the others are less rampant and, in a few cases, repeat flowering. Whichever tendency they display, this is an excellent group of roses with few having a weakness to disease; although those that do are true martyrs.

'Albéric Barbier'

This is one of the best ramblers available in terms of health and freedom of flower and one of the most successful at remaining evergreen. Foliage is dark and glossy, an ideal foil for shapely white-tinged lemon flowers. Growth is pliable and easily trained. Although technically summer-flowering, a mature plant will give the occasional repeat bloom.
Barbier, France, 1900,
summer flowering,
15 x 10 ft. (4.5 x 3 m)

'Albertine'

This is one of the best known roses of all, and, although truly charming, it is also sadly one of the least resistant to disease. Having said this, its susceptibility to mildew and, in my experience, rust can be controlled with sprays provided they are employed before disease strikes, which is not usually until after the flowers have passed. Albertine has beautiful, blowsy, salmon pink flowers that fade with age to near blush. They are very heavily scented. It has gorgeous plum-colored young shoots and leaves and is relatively vigorous.
Barbier, France, 1921,
summer flowering,
4.5 x 3m (15 x 10ft)

'Dorothy Perkins'

This is another famous old variety found in many gardens. Flowers are small, clear pink, scented and are borne in bunches on arching branches. Leaves are small and glossy but sadly rather prone to mildew after flowering. There are several similar varieties available such as crimson 'Excelsa' and the deeper pink 'Minnehaha' all of which are commonly available as weeping standards.
Jackson and Perkins,
USA, 1902,
summer flowering,
10 x 8 ft. (3 x 2.5 m)

'Ethel'

I include 'Ethel' as a very useful rose. Its climbing capabilities are to be marveled at as it can reach great heights in a short time in comparison to other roses. Flowers are small and cupped, but are produced in large trusses against glossy leaves and well-armed branches. It is a seedling of 'Dorothy Perkins,' but does not share its readiness to fall prey to disease. Some nurseries list a variety by the name of 'Belvedere,' and it is possible that they are one and the same rose.
Turner, UK, 1912,
summer flowering,
20 x 15 ft. (6.x 4.5 m)

'Evangeline'

Semisingle blooms are creamy white flushed pink at petal edges' and are borne in large trusses a little later in the summer than many ramblers. Leaves are large and leathery on a strong growing, relatively vigorous plant.
Walsh, USA, 1906,
summer flowering,
20 x 15 ft. (6.x 4.5 m)

'Gardenia'

This has to be one of my all-time favorite roses. The flowers are not individually large or stunning but when in full flush they almost obliterate the dark glossy foliage and fill the air with a fruity aroma. Their coloring is best described as cream to buff, fading slightly with age and they are slightly ragged with many smallish petals.
Manda, USA, 1899,
summer flowering,
20 x 15 ft. (6.x 4.5 m)

'New Dawn'

This is probably the most all-round well-tested climber you will find. There are others that share its generosity of flower, health, and perfume but they have been around for a shorter time and are less well known. It is a sport of the rose 'Dr. Van Fleet,' introduced in the U.S. in 1930, to which it is identical in all respects but remontancy of flower. Buds are plump and open to reveal soft pink, semidouble, pointed and perfumed blooms that become almost flat before falling. Leaves are dark and glossy, and stems bear average quantities of thorns. Growth is not hugely vigorous but ample enough to cover most supports with ease. This is an outstanding rose in all respects, except that because it does all that is asked of a rose by every gardener everywhere, it lacks the quality of being truly outstanding in any one respect. If you have a smaller garden and need a bit of everything in a climber then this is the rose to go for.
Somerset Rose Co.,
USA, 1930,
continuous flowering,
10 x 8 ft. (3 x 2.5 m)

'Sanders White'

Dark glossy foliage and pliable growth are just some of the merits of this rambler. Flowers are small in nodding clusters with the occasional solitary bloom, white, and double. A healthy variety of medium vigor that will give good coverage whether grown against a wall or on a pillar.
Sanders and Sons,
UK, 1912,
summer flowering,
12 x 8 ft. (3.8 x 2.5 m)

Opposite: The dark leaves of 'Gardenia' are a contrasting foil for the fruity scented flowers.

Further

Information

Recommended Roses for Specific Situations

When considering the roses to include in a garden, there may be specific requirements, such as perfume or difficult positions, that need filling. The following lists may be of some help, although due to space restrictions they are in no way fully complete. All can be found in the Directory but many other suitable varieties are available.

FOR SHADED PLACES

Roses prefer to have some light available to them, but can thrive in dappled shade or a place that is shaded for a portion of the day. If there is a position in the garden that would benefit by the inclusion of a rose, the following are good candidates.

SHRUB AND BUSH ROSES

'Alba Semi-Plena'
'Buff Beauty'
'Mme Isaac Pereire'
'Regensberg'
'Westerland'

CLIMBERS AND RAMBLERS

'City of York'
'Félicité Perpétue'
'Gardenia'
'Golden Showers'
'Souvenir du Docteur'
'Jamain'

CLIMBERS AND RAMBLERS FOR NORTH-FACING WALLS

It is inevitable that many of us have these but in all but the severest of winters when they may suffer some die back, the following will cope.

'Blush Noisette'
'Ghislaine de Féligonde'
'Iceberg Climber'
'Mme Alfred Carriere'
'New Dawn'

FOR POOR SOILS

Not all roses will tolerate very poor soil, but there are a few that cope quite well. Do all possible to improve the soil before planting however.

SHRUB AND BUSH ROSES

'Belle Poitevine'
'Celestial'
'Comte de Chambord'
'Fantin Latour'
'Margaret Merril'

CLIMBERS AND RAMBLERS

'Albéric Barbier'
'Leverkusen'
'Mme Caroline Testout'
'Paul's Himalayan Musk'
'Veilchenblau'

FOR ORNAMENTAL VALUE OF HIPS

Roses should be considered for providing color other than that of their flowers. The following varieties set good hips and in some cases will show autumn color in their foliage also. Although some modern bush roses will produce hips, the majority will have been removed during the process of dead-heading. Therefore they are not the best candidates if a stunning display is desired.

SHRUB ROSES

'Mary Queen Of Scots'
Rosa glauca
'Lord Penzance'
Rosa virginiana
'Scabrosa'

CLIMBERS AND RAMBLERS

'Kiftsgate'
'Mme Grégoire Staechelin'
'Rambling Rector'
Rosa helenae
Rosa mulliganii

SHRUB ROSES FOR HEDGING

While a couple of the roses mentioned below are rugosas it is fair to say that nearly all of that group are good hedging plants. Those listed below are all dense and tidy in growth, ideal for a formal hedge.

'Blanc Double de Coubert'
'Roseraie de l'Haÿ'
'Queen Elizabeth'
'Felicia'
'Maiden's Blush Great'

SHORT TO MEDIUM GROWING PILLAR ROSES

Not all climbers are good candidates for a pillar. Those that grow best in such a situation are of less vigor with upright growth. Try one of the following:

'Aloha'
'Dublin Bay'
'Eden Rose '88'
'Golden Showers'
'Kathleen Harrop'

VIGOROUS RAMBLERS FOR CLIMBING THROUGH TREES

If you wish to grow a rose through the branches of trees or over tumble down over eyesores, it will have to have great prowess as a climber. Those below are ideal.

'Ethel'
'Kiftsgate'
'Rambling Rector'
Rosa mulliganii
'Sir Cedric Morris'

FOR FLOWERS OVER A LONG PEROID

While once-flowering roses usually provide the most stunning displays, there are roses that will flower well into the autumn.

SHRUB AND BUSH ROSES

'Bonica '82'
'Felicia'
'Jacqueline du Pré'
'Macmillan Nurse'
'Norwich Castle'

CLIMBERS AND RAMBLERS

'Aloha'
'Dublin Bay'
'Gloire de Dijon'
'Mme Alfred Carriere'
'New Dawn'

FOR PERFUME

For some people a rose must be perfumed to have garden value, but not all roses are. The following are all well scented in my opinion, but this is a controversial issue. The scent of a particular variety may appeal to many, but to others seem devoid of any perfume at all.

SHRUB AND BUSH ROSES

'Anna Pavlova'
'Comte de Chambord'
'Ferdinand Pichard'
'Kazanlik'
'Mme Isaac Pereire'

CLIMBERS AND RAMBLERS

'Aloha'
'Blairii No.2'
'Gardenia'
'Gloire de Dijon'
'Sombreuil'

FOR THE SMALLER GARDEN

Not everyone has the space for large shrub roses or towering climbers. Those listed below are compact in habit and should not outgrow their welcome. The climbers and ramblers are easily controlled. All these roses are also candidates for growing in containers.

SHRUB AND BUSH ROSES

'Alfred de Dalmas'
'Comte de Chambord'
'Rose de Meaux'
'Sweet Dream'
'Twenty-fifth'

CLIMBERS AND RAMBLERS

'Aloha'
'Blush Noisette'
'Ghislaine de Féligonde'
'Narrow Water'
'Zéphirine Drouhin'

FOR WILD GARDENS AND WOODLAND

When planting roses in such situations it is best to choose those that will not only complement the area but which will cope well if not tended to often. Ramblers work well through the branches of trees or if just left to tumble over the ground.

SHRUB ROSES

'Common Moss'
'Grouse'
Rosa canina
Rosa glauca
Rosa virginiana

RAMBLERS

'Kiftsgate'
'Rambling Rector'
Rosa arvensis
Rosa helenae
Rosa wichuraiana

Rose Societies

Both the American and British Rose Societies are large bodies with membership advantages. They produce regular publications and offer advice to members should they need it.

UNITED KINGDOM
THE ROYAL NATIONAL ROSE SOCIETY
Chiswell Green, St Albans, Hertfordshire, AL2 2NR

UNITED STATES
THE AMERICAN ROSE SOCIETY
PO Box 30,000, Shreveport, Louisiana, 71130

HERITAGE ROSE FOUNDATION
1512 Gorman Street, Raleigh, North Carolina 27606

Bibliography

Beales, Amanda. *Old Fashioned Roses*, Cassell, 1990
Beales, Amanda. *Rose Basics*, Hamlyn, 1999
Beales, Peter. *Classic Roses*, revised edition, Harvill, 1997
Beales, Peter. *Roses*, HarperCollins, 1992
Beales, Peter. *Twentieth Century Roses*, Collins Harvill,1988
Jekyll, Gertrude, and Mawley, Edward. *Roses for English Gardens*, Antique Collectors Club, reprinted 1990
Le Rougetel, Hazel. *A Heritage of Roses*, Unwin Hyman, 1988
Paterson, Allen. *The History of the Rose*, Collins, 1983
Royal National Rose Society. *How to Grow Roses*, 1992
Scanniello, Stephen, and Bayard, Tania. *Roses of America*, Henry Holt, 1990
Squire, David. *Roses*, Hamlyn, 1998
Thomas, Graham Stuart. *The Old Shrub Roses*, Dent, 1986
Toogood, Alan. *Propagation*, Dent, 1980
Various authors. *Botanica's Roses (The Encyclopedia Of Roses)*, Grange Books, 1998

Glossary

Acidity
A state of the soil where the pH is less than 7.

Alkaline
A state of the soil where the pH is more than 7.

Anther
The part of the stamen containing pollen.

Bare-rooted
The term describing roses dug up and sold without the benefit of being potted.

Bud
The unopened flower.

Budding
A form of propagation involving the placing of a scion into a rootstock.

Calyx
The green leaves protecting the flower in bud.

Cambium
A layer of growth cells immediately below the bark.

Chlorosis
The discoloring of leaves associated with deficiencies.

Cluster
A group of flowers together from one stem.

Continuous flowering
Flowers appear successively throughout the season.

Division
A form of propagation involving the transplanting of suckers.

Emasculation
The removal of all male parts of the flower during hybridization.

Fertilization
The fusion of the male pollen with the ovule of the female parent in order to produce seed.

Fibrous root
The hairy parts of rose roots, with most growth activity.

Germination
The term used to describe the appearance of a seedling from a fertilized seed.

Glaucous
A gray to blue coloring.

Grafting
A method of propagation where material from one rose is encouraged to bond with the roots of another.

Heel
The small piece of two-year-old bark found at the base of heel cuttings.

Heeling-in
A method of storing bare-rooted roses in the ground before planting.

Hip
The seed-carrying fruit of roses.

Hybrid
A variety that is derived from two other roses.

Hybridization
The method of creating new rose varieties.

Lax
An open, loose habit of growth.

Layering
A method of propagation involving burying a section of a branch while still growing roots develop.

Moss
The hairy down found on some roses

Mulch
An application of usually organic material spread over the ground.

Node
The place at a leaf joint where a bud is found.

Nutrient
A water-soluble beneficial substance found in the soil and taken up by the roots.

Pegging-down
A way of training shrub roses so that they are broad in growth.

pH
The scale on which alkalinity and acidity are measured in the soil.

Pollinate
The application of male pollen to the female stigma of a separate flower during hybridization.

Procumbent
A manner of growth being broader than tall.

Pruning
The cutting back of plants to encourage young growth and improved flowering.

Receptacle
The swollen area found at the base of the flower, which will later become the hip

Reflexed
A flower form where the petals furl back on the open flower.

Repeat flowering
Flowers appear in definite waves during the season.

Rootstock
The rose used for the host roots on budded and grafted plants.

Scion
The piece of plant stem used in budding and grafting which will become the branches of the plant, attached to the rootstock.

Seedling
An un-named variety of rose, often awaiting introduction.

Spine
A long, narrow sharp thorn.

Spore
The seed of fungal diseases.

Sport
A variety which has come about as a mutation on another rose.

Stamen
Stamens make up the whorl, which surrounds the stigma within a flower.

Stigma
The very centre of the rose with receptive cells prepared to accept pollen.

Suckers
The branches that grow from roots separate from the main plant.

Summer flowering
Flowering just once during the summer.

Tap root
The main and thickest roots of the root system

Union
The place on a budded or grafted plant where branches and roots join.

Index

INDEX

127

Photographic acknowledgments

Acknowledgements in Source Order

AKG, London/Archiv fuer Kunst and Geschichte
16,/Gilles Mermet 12 top
Peter Beales 8,79
Bridgeman Art Library, London/Giraudon 17,/Walker
Art Gallery, Liverpool 14 top
Corbis UK Ltd/Bettmann 13 bottom
E.T. Archive 10-11, 13 top, 18
Garden Picture Library 45 top,/Mark Bolton
19,/Howard Rice 6-7,20-21
Octopus Publishing Group Ltd./Sean Myers 32-33, 34,
35 top right, 35 bottom left, 38-39, 42 top, 42 bottom,
43 top, 43 centre, 43 bottom, 45 bottom, 48 top, 48 bottom, 49 top, 50, 51 top, 52-53, 56, 57 top left, 57 top
right, 70,
/Mark Winwood back cover, front endpaper, back endpaper, 1, 2-3, 4-5, 9, 14 bottom left, 14 bottom right, 22
top right, 22 bottom left, 23 top, 24, 25 top left, 25 bottom left, 25 bottom right, 26, 27, 28-29, 30 top, 30 bottom, 31, 32 top left, 33 top right, 36, 37, 40, 44, 46, 47
Top, 47 bottom, 49 bottom, 51 bottom, 54, 55, 58, 59,
61, 62, 63, 64-65, 66, 67, 68 top, 68 bottom, 69, 71, 72,
73 top, 73 bottom, 74-75, 77, 78, 81, 82, 85, 86, 87, 88,
90, 91, 92 left, 92 right, 93, 94, 95, 96, 98 top left, 98
bottom right, 99, 100, 101, 102 top, 102 bottom, 103,
104, 105, 106 top, 106 bottom, 107, 108, 109 top, 109
bottom, 110, 111, 112 top, 112 bottom, 113, 114, 115, 116
top, 116 bottom, 117, 119, 120-121,/Steve Wooster front
cover